Governor T.A. Osborn

The State Government and the Indian Bureau

The Osage troubles in Barbour County, Kansas, in the summer of 1874.

Correspondence between the state government and the Interior

department; testimony relative to the killing of four Osage Indians

Governor T.A. Osborn

The State Government and the Indian Bureau
*The Osage troubles in Barbour County, Kansas, in the summer of 1874.
Correspondence between the state government and the Interior department;
testimony relative to the killing of four Osage Indians*

ISBN/EAN: 9783337307752

Printed in Europe, USA, Canada, Australia, Japan

Cover: Foto ©Suzi / pixelio.de

More available books at **www.hansebooks.com**

THE STATE GOVERNMENT AND THE INDIAN BUREAU.

THE OSAGE TROUBLES

IN BARBOUR COUNTY, KANSAS,

IN THE SUMMER OF 1874.

CORRESPONDENCE BETWEEN THE STATE GOVERNMENT AND THE INTE-
RIOR DEPARTMENT—TESTIMONY RELATIVE TO THE
KILLING OF FOUR OSAGE INDIANS.

TOPEKA, KANSAS:
GEO. W. MARTIN, KANSAS PUBLISHING HOUSE.
1875.

THE OSAGE INDIAN TROUBLES
IN KANSAS.

CORRESPONDENCE.

MEDICINE LODGE, BARBOUR COUNTY, KAS., }
June 17, 1874. }

Hon. T. A. Osborn, Governor State of Kansas:

SIR: The Indians are raiding Barbour county, and have this day killed one of our citizens, that we know of, and probably more.

Kiowa was attacked yesterday, and a number of horses run off. Four tribes are on the war-path, and threaten to clean out the Medicine river country.

The lives of the people are in danger. We need immediate assistance.

(Signed)·

WM. M. FRIEDLEY.	B. H. REED.
G. W. ELLIS.	C. T. RIGG.
O. D. MERRIMAN.	J. R. EASLEY.
REV. G. W. KELLER.	W. F. CRISP.
H. JONES.	H. MORE.
A. WINSTON.	J. MORE.

P. S.—Mr. Keim, a farmer living near Medicine Lodge, was killed and scalped yesterday, one mile and a half from here.

REPORT OF COMMITTEE.

MEDICINE LODGE, BARBOUR COUNTY, KAS., }
June 19, 1874. }

Hon. Thomas A. Osborn, Governor of Kansas:

The undersigned, appointed by the unanimous voice of the people of Barbour county to represent to you the state of affairs, so far as Indians are concerned, in this county, make the following statement:

1st. On the 16th of June the Indians attacked Davis's Ranch, capturing seven horses. After an engagement, they drove the citizens into their houses and carried off their plunder.

2d. Attacked settlements in the vicinity of Medicine Lodge; killed, scalped and mutilated three citizens, to wit: Isaac Keim, J. Martin, and Elijah Kennedy, peaceable and law-abiding men, two of whom had large families; and, in addition, they stole two good teams, the property of the murdered men.

3d. The Indians were Arapahoes or Cheyennes—probably the latter.

4th. The people are greatly alarmed; need rations and arms to enable them to protect their homes, and this immediately.

All of which is respectfully submitted.

(Signed)　　　　　　M. W. SUTTON, Co. Att'y,
　　　　　　　　　　B. P. AYERS,
　　　　　　　　　　JACOB SWANK,
　　　　　　　　　　　　　　Committee.

P. S.—From reliable information, we are satisfied that the Cheyennes, Arapahoes and Osages have consolidated for hostile purposes.　　　M. W. SUTTON,
　　　　　　　　　　　B. P. AYERS,
　　　　　　　　　　　JACOB SWANK,
　　　　　　　　　　　　　Committee.

MEDICINE LODGE, June 20.

CAPT. MORRIS—*Dear Sir:* You probably know by this time that since you left we have had *business* here. The facts are these:

1st. Three scalped heads (and bodies) have been brought into town, buried, etc.

2d. They were killed by Indians.

3d. The whole country is alarmed, and men cannot work, consequently cannot support their families.

4th. They have moved into town with their families.

5th. They will need subsistence.

6th. They can protect themselves, if their families can be fed and they be organized.

7th. They wish IMMEDIATE answer.

　　　　　　Yours, etc.,　　　B. P. AYERS.

BARBOUR COUNTY, KANSAS, }
SUN CITY, June 21, 1874. }

Hon. Mr. Osborn, Governor State of Kansas:

DEAR SIR: The people of Barbour county are suffering from Indian raids. Many horses have been stolen, and five men have been found killed and scalped by them. Most of the settlers will leave the county unless the State can give them protection.

Yours in haste, from

S. B. DOUGLASS,
Co. Supt. Pub. Instruction of Barbour Co.

MEDICINE LODGE, BARBOUR CO., KANSAS, }
June 25, 1874. }

Gov. Thos. A. Osborn, Topeka, Kansas:

We, the undersigned citizens of Barbour county, State of Kansas, respectfully ask that a military company be organized, and that Cyrus M. Ricker, of Medicine Lodge, be appointed and commissioned captain of said company.

WM. M. FRIEDLEY.	BYRON P. AYERS.
W. H. ROUST.	C. P. W. ELLIS.
W. F. CRISP.	M. L. BOURMAN.
JAMES T. WHITELAW.	JACOB RHIAN.
G. W. EBERSOLE.	M. S. COBB.
M. D. HOUK.	H. H. BEDFORD.
C. W. LUCAS.	T. F. SHEPLER.
W. E. LUCAS.	W. E. WYATT.
CHARLES PARSONS.	C. WEIDNER.
CLARK GILLMORE.	T. F. MARQUAND.
B. T. LAMPTON.	J. R. EASLEY.
A. V. SHEPLER.	A. H. IZARD.
WM. M. LAMPTON.	JOHN CASTINE.
J. N. LANE.	W. SIMS.
I. W. STUTSMAN.	J. G. MOORE.
B. H. REED.	J. H. ANDERSON.
T. W. DAVIS.	JAMES TAYLOR.
A. A. WILBER.	L. J. WILKERSON.
J. W. MOORE.	T. W. McCLURE.
L. WYATT.	JOHN C. BONER.
D. F. LUCAS.	M. VAN SLYLER.
GEORGE P. LUCAS.	FREDERICK VERNING.
H. A. MOORE.	FRANK McALISTER.
R. CONABLE.	ANDREW BARNES.
G. POSTELWAIGHT.	JOHN BEELER.
JOHN W. UPPERMAN,	E. W. ILIFF.
JAMES F. WEAVER.	T. F. SHEPLER.

MEDICINE LODGE, BARBOUR COUNTY, KAS., }
July 1, 1874.   }

Hon. Thomas A. Osborn, Governor State of Kansas:

DEAR SIR: The bearer hereof, Cyrus Ricker, is a man in every way worthy of respect and confidence, and I hope that, for the safety of our people here, there will be no hesitancy in granting the request of the people of this place. Something must be done for our defense, or we must perish, together with our women and children, as it is utterly impossible for many to get away.

Very respectfully,

WILLIAM M. FRIEDLEY.

[TELEGRAM.]

HEADQUARTERS DEPARTMENT OF THE MISSOURI, }
FORT LEAVENWORTH, KAS., July 10, 1874.   }

To Governor T. A. Osborn, Topeka, Kas.:

*   *   *   *   *   *   *   *   *   *   *

[Extract.]

Cavalry I cannot spare from the protection of the southern frontier of Kansas without endangering the safety of the people.

(Signed)   JOHN POPE,

Brevet Major General Commanding.

[NOTE.—The United States troops were withdrawn about the last of July, to accompany General Miles's Expedition.]

WELLINGTON, KAS., July 22, 1874.

GOV. OSBORN—*Dear Sir:* I am sorry that I was detained at Winfield, as I desired to see you. As you have seen for yourself, much damage has already been done by the Indian scare. It seems to me that it is for the best interests of the State that this should not be repeated. While there may be no danger, yet prudence dictates that some security should be given to our people, and that security should be our own men, organized into companies. One company of men organized at this point would do more to restore confidence than half a dozen companies of United States forces, who may be ordered elsewhere at any moment, and thus leave us unprotected. That the Indians are dangerous you must admit. They may not bother us; yet they might;—and you could hardly justify yourself in case some of our people should be murdered, by saying that you were desirous to save the expense necessary in ordering this company into active service. My judgment for it is that it will be acting wisely for you to order this company out at once, and keep them for at least ninety days. It can do no harm, and may be the means of saving valuable lives and property.

I have no interest in writing this other than to secure sure protection for our women and children. I could not ask for more. It seems to be necessary to our people. It can do no harm, and justice to our border demands it.

I hope you will grant my request in this matter at once, and I, as well as the people of this county, will feel that you have placed us under lasting obligations to you.

Hoping to hear from you favorably, at your earliest convenience, I am, yours truly,

WM. P. HACKNEY.

OFFICE OF CLERK OF SUMNER COUNTY, }
WELLINGTON, KANSAS, July 23, 1874. }

Gov. T. A. OSBORN—*Dear Sir:* Our settlers continue to leave on account of Indian war rumors. They do not seem to have confidence in the U. S. troops, as there is a liability of their being ordered away at any time. Under this condition of things, and to reassure the people and restore confidence, my opinion is, it would be well to call the company here into service. I think if some of our own men were stationed west of us, settlers would then go back to their homes satisfied, and I believe the State can better afford the expenditure than to have the country so depopulated, and immigration stopped. The minds of the settlers are agitated by the stories set afloat, whether with or without foundation, and they will not rest satisfied until a feeling of greater security prevails. Truly yours,

C. S. BRODBENT,
County Clerk.

MEDICINE LODGE, BARBOUR COUNTY, KAS., }
July 24, 1874. }

SIR: I have the honor to acknowledge the receipt of commission as "Captain of Company A, Barbour County Militia;" also that of *one* of my lieutenants.

The commissions came to me through Sheriff Collins, of Reno county.

I have no other means of knowing whether you received the communication accompanying roster, etc.

I deem it of much importance to know what our exact position as to *service* is, and hope you may give me any information you can command upon the subject.

The general aspect of affairs is about the same as when I wrote last. One of my scouts reports this evening that he found in the Cedar Mountains, about ten miles southeast of this post, on yesterday, two wagons loaded with cedar timber. The teams had been cut from the wagons, and everything seemed to indicate that the animals (two mules and two horses) had been taken and the drivers captured. The wagons are old—one without a bed. The one with a bed was painted red. The "outfit" is not known in this vicinity, and is supposed to have belonged in some other county. It might be well enough to give publicity to the matter through the press.

Hoping to hear from you soon,

I remain, your obedient servant,

C. M. RICKER,
Captain Commanding Co. A, Barbour Co. Militia.

To the Adjutant General, State of Kansas.

[The foregoing communications are published simply as samples of a very voluminous correspondence, showing the necessity of a militia force in the southwest.]

CAPTAIN RICKER'S REPORT OF THE ENGAGEMENT OF AUGUST 7, 1874.

HEADQUARTERS Co. A, KANSAS STATE MILITIA, }
MEDICINE LODGE, BARBOUR Co., AUG. 7, 1874. }

C. A. Morris, Adj. Gen'l State of Kansas, Topeka:

SIR: I have the honor to state that on my return from Wichita, I found the people were greatly excited over the rumors that were coming in daily of more and more Indians being seen around us, and that from their actions they were all on the war-path.

A few days ago, forty of them made their appearance in front of the stockade at Kiowa, sixteen miles south of this point, where I have twenty-five of my men on duty, and examined the location of the same very closely. From there they moved east and north, through the Cedar Hills. From what I can learn, they are the same band that captured two teams from Wiggins a short time since. They set fire to and burned off all the range on their route.

To satisfy myself in regard to the correctness and truth of these reports, I, with Lieut. Moseley and twenty-five men, left Medicine Lodge this morning, and traveled northeast about fifteen miles, where I encountered between forty and fifty young braves of the Osage tribe. Six of them advanced towards us, while the balance formed for battle on a hill south of us. I halted my command and made signs for the forward ones to advance, which they did, coming up to us with their bows strung and arrows in their hands, guns and revolvers cocked. I ordered them to give up their arms. Three of them did so, the other three refusing to understand me. I then (through Lieut. Moseley, who acted as interpreter) requested them to have the braves dismount and advance; but in place of this (thinking, perhaps, that we could not understand them), they ordered them not to come, but to fire into my men, which was immediately done; the others then made a dash to stampede my horses.

We then commenced firing on them, and had an exciting time for a few moments. The Indians retreated south, and not having force enough I was unable to pursue them far, as they had reinforcements close at hand, and I thought it prudent to return, which I did in safety. I had one man severely wounded in the head; the Indians lost five killed and several wounded. I captured some mules and ponies from them. The Indians were all young men, and the horses they rode were in fine condition.

General, it requires one hundred pounds of flour daily to feed my men; besides that, there are twenty families here that I am obliged to issue rations to. I want to know whether you are going to help us or not: we must have provisions and ammunition immediately.

Inclosed you will find the enrollment papers of recruits of my command. Please answer me through Capt. Tucker, at Wichita. I will send teams there to-day for supplies.

I have the honor to be, very respectfully,
Your obedient servant,
C. M. RICKER, *Capt. Commanding.*

MEDICINE LODGE, BARBOUR COUNTY, KAS., }
September 10, 1874. }

SIR: I inclose herewith an additional report—accompanied by affidavits—of my operations on and about the 7th of August last, with the Osage Indians.

The stock captured consisted of forty-one ponies, serviceable and unserviceable; four mules, serviceable; two mules, unserviceable; four sucking colts. No other property of value was found. The ponies captured were of inferior quality and small value.

The previous report—together with papers herewith transmitted—demonstrate conclusively to me—

1st. The Indians were Osages.

2d. They were outside of their territorial limits.

3d. They were on a marauding, if not a *murdering*, expedition.

4th. They committed the first overt act of hostility.

In this connection I can state that, among frontiersmen and others best qualified to judge of such matters, the opinion is universal that the tribes of Great and Little Osages were guilty of the murder of Keim, Martin, and Kennedy.

I do not wish that any action of the Commander-in-Chief, in the premises, should directly or indirectly stigmatize me or my command as murderers or thieves, as is desired by Gibson or Stubbs.   Respectfully,

C. M. RICKER, *Captain.*

To the Adjutant General, State of Kansas.

P. S.—A portion of the command engaged in the Osage affair are on detached duty.   C. M. R.

AFFIDAVITS OF CAPT. RICKER AND OTHERS.

STATE OF KANSAS, COUNTY OF BARBOUR.

Cyrus M. Ricker, being duly sworn, deposes and says: On the 7th day of August, 1874, and previous to that time, I was Captain of Company "A," Barbour County Militia. I received intelligence on the 6th that a body of Osage Indians were camped in the county eighteen miles northeast of this post. Being informed that parties from Sumner county had been robbed of their horses—*vide* previous report—by Osages in that vicinity, I detailed twenty-three men on the 7th and started for their camp for the purpose of causing them to leave the county for the Territory, by force if necessary.

Upon arriving in the neighborhood of the Indians, I concealed my men in a ravine and advanced alone to a point within one hundred and fifty (150) yards of the Indians, where I was met by one in a hostile attitude, followed by eight or ten others; four were disarmed partially, when one gave the command to the remainder, who were in line in the rear, to fire, which they did. My command returned the fire, and the result was five dead Indians.

I took possession of their ponies and returned to this point the same day.

[SEAL.]   C. M. RICKER.

Subscribed and sworn to this —— day of September, A. D. 1874.   M. D. HOUK, *County Clerk.*

B. L. Lampton, W. M. Lampton, Henry Bedford, A. A. Wilber and J. M. Stutsman, being duly sworn according to law, depose and say that they have read the foregoing statement, and that the matters and things set forth therein are true and correct; that they were members of said militia company, and present at the time of the conflict reported herein.

WM. M. LAMPTON.
B. L. LAMPTON.
J. M. STUTSMAN.
A. A. WILBER.
H. BEDFORD.

STATE OF KANSAS, COUNTY OF BARBOUR.

Before me, M. D. Houk, County Clerk of said county, this day personally appeared the parties whose names are above attached, to me well known as truthful men, and subscribed and swore to the said statement.

Witness my hand and the seal of said county, this 10th day of September, 1874.

[SEAL.]   M. D. HOUK, *County Clerk.*

LETTER FROM A. C. WILLIAMS, SPECIAL AGENT OF THE KICKAPOOS.

ARKANSAS CITY, KAS., Sept. 1, 1874.

SIR: I have the honor to report that this morning, as I was proceeding from this place to my special agency on Shawkaska creek, I met two of my Kickapoo Indians, who informed me that a party of Little Osages came to the agency last night and inquired for me, and behaved in such a manner that most of the Kickapoos became alarmed and took to the woods. The Osages, however, said they would not injure any of the red people, but will kill any and all whites they may find in the Territory. The Kickapoos are alarmed, and ask protection from the whites, or to be removed up to the State line. In order to supply my Indians with provisions, and to make some arrangements for their protection or removal, and for the temporary protection of Government property, I would request an escort from your company of Kansas State Militia.

A. C. WILLIAMS, *Special Agent.*

To Capt. G. H. Norton, Comdg. Co. A, Cowley Co. Mounted Militia.

AFFIDAVIT OF AYLMER D. KEITH.

STATE OF KANSAS, COWLEY COUNTY, ss.

I, Aylmer D. Keith, being first duly sworn, say that on the 17th day of August, 1874, in conversation with Mahlon Stubbs, late agent of the Kaws, said Stubbs used the following language, in regard to the anticipated troubles with the Osage Indians, to wit: "The Indians have held a council and declared for war; they are on the fight the biggest kind. In my opinion, you are in ten times as much danger as you ever have been."

AYLMER D. KEITH.

COWLEY COUNTY, STATE OF KANSAS, ss.

Subscribed and sworn to before me, this 1st day of September, 1874.   JAMES L. HUEY,
Notary Public.

AFFIDAVIT OF C. M. SCOTT.

STATE OF KANSAS, COWLEY COUNTY, ss.

C. M. Scott, being duly sworn, deposes and says that the following statement is, to the best of his knowledge, just and correct:

Wednesday, February 18, 1874, two Osages belonging to "Hard Robe's" band of Indians came into Arkansas City, and stopped at my office. "Stanislaw," or Och-tun-ba-ka, I think belongs properly to Chetopa's band. He is a good interpreter, and speaks English plainly. He said he had dispatches for several agents, and was on that errand. Nan-hunk-gah, the man with him, was sent in by Hard Robe to have some one bring out provisions to him on the Shawkaska, where he was then camped. The Indians stayed with me all night, sleeping in the office, as we were always friendly. In conversing, they told me they were going on a buffalo hunt soon, and as they had frequently invited me to accompany them, I thought it a little strange they should seem to avoid speaking of it this time; so I asked Stanislaw, and he said to go with him the next time.

I said, "I guess I'll go with you this time."

He said, "Maybe so the Indians wouldn't like it."

I asked, "Why not?"

He said, "Maybe we fight."

I said, "Do you mean you are going on the war-path?"

He said, "Maybe we kill some one."

I said, "Do you mean to kill a white man?"

He said, "No, we kill a Cheyenne."

I told him I would as lieve go on the war path myself with them, if they were only going to kill Indians, and that I wanted to go.

He said the Indians wouldn't like it, but that it would be all right the next time. And in further conversation, he told me some one of the Osages had died, and that they would have a scalp. I think it was a young squaw, for he said they would not kill an old man, or one with *gray* hair; but that it must be a young man, or one whose hair was not gray.

Sometime in the latter part of May or first of June I saw Stanislaw again, and told him I heard they were going out again, and that I would go this time sure. That I would ride to their camp on the Shawkaska, and join them. He was very sullen, and said but little. About this time I published a warning through the columns of the Arkansas City *Traveler*, intimating that it would not be safe to be on the plains, and that if caught I would not give much for their hair. Previous to this, one "Jim" had told Capt. Norton that the Osages were mad, and intended raiding on Arkansas City, and advised the captain with his family to leave.

Sometime in June (I think the 10th day), one William Wilson, in the employ of the L., L. & G. R. R., to run a ferry across the Arkansas at Deer Creek, and a resident of this county, was coming in from a trip west, where he had been to look after cattle, and on a creek not far from the Kickapoo

Agency, saw a party of Osages painted black, and knowing it meant "no good," avoided them, although he was well acquainted with them, and fearing trouble he went immediately to the Kickapoo Agency, and informed them what he had seen; when he was told that Stanislaw had been there and made some statements. He then came to my office and told me of it, and wanted to raise a company of ten or more picked men to follow them, make an attack by surprise and bring them back. I remarked that would be about as good a way to get into the Kansas Penitentiary as I knew of, and persuaded him to abandon the idea.

O. P. Johnson, now in the employ of the United States as a scout at Cheyenne Agency, was in town, and I told him what Stanislaw had said and Wilson had seen, and he began estimating and said, "Within ten days some one would lose their hair." If I remember right, he missed his calculation by three days.

It was generally known that the Osages hated the Moseleys and Leonard on Medicine Lodge, and Johnson and all conceded they would make trouble on that creek before any other. At this place even, an Osage hanging around Medicine Lodge would have been considered suspicious.

From February 18, 1874, I have regarded the Osages as very much dissatisfied and dangerous, and from the date of Wilson's statement, June 10, 1874, I have regarded them as being bent on killing white persons, or on the war-path, as I think has been definitely demonstrated, at least to the people of the border, who are generally aware of the facts. The main reason for our people denouncing Agent Gibson, was that he permitted these people to go off on an errand of this kind without notifying them in any manner whatever.   C. M. SCOTT.

Sworn and subscribed to before me, a justice of the peace of Creswell township, in and for Cowley county, State of Kansas, this 30th day of August, 1874.   J. H. BONSELL,
Justice of the Peace.

CORRESPONDENCE BETWEEN THE GOVERNOR AND SECRETARY OF THE INTERIOR.

DEPARTMENT OF THE INTERIOR, }
WASHINGTON, D. C., December 7, 1874. }

SIR: On the receipt, by this Department, of information from the Commissioner of Indian Affairs of the alleged murder, by Kansas militia, of five Osage Indians, in Barbour county, Kas., a commission was appointed, consisting of F. H. Smith, J. W. Smith, and Wilson Shannon, to investigate the facts and circumstances in relation to the killing of said Indians.

A copy of the report of the commission upon the subject is herewith transmitted for your information and consideration.

To the last two paragraphs of said report your attention is particularly invited. They contain recommendations which I respectfully express the hope you may find it consistent with your sense of public duty to carry into effect, especially in view of the fact that this Department is precluded, for the want of appropriate funds, from making any compensation to the Osages on account of the losses they have sustained by the unfortunate occurrence referred to.

The testimony, somewhat voluminous, is on file in this Department, a copy of which will be forwarded, if you desire it.

Very respectfully,

Your obedient servant,

C. DELANO, *Secretary.*

To Hon. Thomas A. Osborn, Governor of Kansas, Topeka, Kansas.

[The following are the two concluding paragraphs of the report referred to in the foregoing letter:

"For the purpose of this report, the organization termed 'Militia' has been treated as a force acting legally under the authority of the State of Kansas. It appears, however, that at the date of the occurrence no such authority had vested in them; that the order calling them into the service was not issued until ten days subsequently; and to what extent its ante-date to cover the period of this transaction changes the nature of the conduct of these persons from an act of murder to an act of war, it is not now proposed to inquire.

"It is presumed the authorities of Kansas, when their attention is called to the evidence in the case, will not hesitate to direct the return of the captured property. In the judgment of the commission, the Government of the United States should, in any event, see that the Indians are reimbursed."]

EXECUTIVE DEPARTMENT,
TOPEKA, KANSAS, January 16, 1875.

Hon. C. Delano, Secretary of the Interior, Washington, D. C.:

SIR: I have the honor to acknowledge the receipt of your communication of the 7th ultimo, inclosing a copy of the report of a commission appointed by your department to investigate the facts and circumstances in relation to the killing of five Osage Indians in Barbour county, Kansas, by the militia of this State.

In reply, I feel it my duty to express my earnest conviction that the commission is entirely in error in its conclusion. Soon after the killing of the Osages referred to, I detailed an officer to visit Barbour county, with instructions to investigate thoroughly the nature of the engagement between the militia and the Indians. The report of the officer (Capt. J. W. Morris) left no doubt in my mind as to the character of the Indians, and the purpose of their presence in that section. The Indians were there for hostile purposes; they made the first attack, and the losses which they sustained were sustained in the engagement which followed the attack. This was, in substance, the report of Capt. Ricker, in command of the company of militia, following the engagement, and the investigation afterwards made by my order fully sustained its truthfulness. Subsequently my Adjutant General, while in Barbour county, made inquiry in regard to the matter, under instructions from me, and his report also fully sustains the conclusions formerly arrived at.

A copy of the Annual Report of the Adjutant General is transmitted herewith, and your attention is respectfully invited to marked passages on pages 9, 10, 11, 13, 14, 15 and 26, and especially to the designated passage commencing on page 10. In this connection, permit me also to call your attention to the list of murders committed by Indians in this State, to be found on pages 34 and 35.

The stock captured upon the occasion referred to has been disposed of by the authority of the State.

I have the honor to be, sir, very respectfully, your obedient servant,   THOMAS A. OSBORN.

[TELEGRAM.]

EXECUTIVE DEPARTMENT, }
TOPEKA, KANSAS, December 24, 1874. }

To the President, Washington, D. C.:

I am informed by Agent Gibson that parties of Osages have left their reservation, ostensibly to hunt. I fear a collision between them and the settlers in the southwestern part of this State, if they are not returned to their reservation.

THOMAS A. OSBORN,
Governor of Kansas.

DEPARTMENT OF THE INTERIOR, }
WASHINGTON, D. C., January 11, 1875. }

SIR: This Department received, by reference from the President, your telegram of the 24th ultimo, relative to certain Osage Indians off reservation.

For your information, I transmit herewith copy of a report, dated the 5th instant, from the Commissioner of Indian Affairs, to whom your communication was referred.

Very respectfully, your obedient servant,

B. R. COWEN, *Acting Secretary.*

Hon. Thomas A. Osborn, Governor of Kansas.

[COPY.]

DEPARTMENT OF THE INTERIOR, }
OFFICE OF INDIAN AFFAIRS, }
WASHINGTON, D. C., January 5, 1875. }

SIR: I have the honor to acknowledge the receipt, by Department reference of December 31, of telegram from his Excellency, Thomas A. Osborn, Governor of Kansas, to the President, stating that he is informed that parties of Osages have left their reservation, ostensibly to hunt, and that he fears collision between them and the settlers in Southwestern Kansas.

Respecting the cause of alarm in the apprehension of Gov. Osborn, I have to state that these Osages are the people, a band of whom were murderously attacked by a party of men—afterwards enrolled by Governor Osborn as Kansas militia—and four of their number brutally killed, and the band plundered of the property they had along with them.

The Osages have repeatedly asked of the Government, and of Governor Osborn, that steps be taken to punish these murderers and return the property. As to the most prompt and efficient

2

method of preventing the Osages from attempting retaliation for the murder of their brethren, I beg to venture the suggestion that it will be found in the putting forth of vigorous efforts on the part of the authorities of Kansas to comply with the manifest requirements simply of justice and humanity. If the agent of the Osages were authorized to assure these Indians that the murderers at Medicine Lodge would be brought to punishment, and their stolen property returned, the Kansas border would be entirely quiet, so far as this tribe is concerned; and until this is done, it will be very difficult, if not impossible, to prevent the Osages from giving occasional causes of alarm to a people who must be conscious of having deeply wronged them.

Very respectfully, your obedient servant,
EDWARD P. SMITH, *Commissioner.*
The Honorable Secretary of the Interior.

DEPARTMENT OF THE INTERIOR, }
WASHINGTON, D. C., July 13, |1875. }

SIR: I have the honor to invite your attention to the accompanying copy of the report of the Commissioner of Indian Affairs, dated the 3d instant, relating to the murder of Osage Indians by citizens of Kansas in August, 1874, which was the subject of Department letter to you dated 7th December, 1874, and of your reply thereto dated January 16th, 1875.

The testimony in possession of this Department, touching the facts of this case, seems conclusive that the act committed by the so-called Kansas Militia was a wanton and unprovoked outrage upon the Osages.

In transmitting the report of the Commissioner of Indian Affairs, I respectfully commend his suggestion to your favorable consideration: that the murderers be punished, or, if that cannot be done, that the State of Kansas restore the stolen property or its equivalent, and make reparation for the murders committed.

I inclose for your information a copy of a letter of this date, addressed to the Commissioner of Indian Affairs, on the subject.

Very respectfully, your obedient servant,
C. DELANO, *Secretary.*
Hon. Thomas A. Osborn, Governor of Kansas, Topeka, Kansas.

[COPY.]

DEPARTMENT OF THE INTERIOR, ⎫
OFFICE OF INDIAN AFFAIRS, ⎬
WASHINGTON, D. C., July 3, 1875. ⎭

SIR: As supplemental to the frequent communications, heretofore, between this office and the Department upon the subject of the outrage committed upon the Osages last August, I feel obliged, in the interests of peace and humanity, as well as the rights of the Indians, to make the following statement as to the condition of affairs at the present time.

One year ago a party of Osage Indians, about thirty in number—men, women and children—belonging to the bands of "Black Dog" and "Big Chief," were peacefully engaged in hunting in the buffalo country, in the southwestern part of Kansas, upon what was a part of their former reservation, when they were attacked by about forty Kansas citizens, under command of one Capt. Ricker, who were afterwards ordered upon duty as militia by the Governor of Kansas, the order being ante-dated so as to cover this outrage. Four of the Osages were murdered, and their property, and that of the other Indians, consisting of sixty ponies, saddles, bridles, blankets, and other camp equipage, was plundered and carried off by the so-called militia. The facts in the case are abundantly sustained by the affidavits of more than fifteen reputable citizens, who were eye-witnesses to the transaction; and on their testimony it is palpably evident that the affair was a cold-blooded murder, followed by theft and robbery. The Osages were greatly incensed at the time, and a border war deemed inevitable; but owing to the influence of the agent, and his promise to them that the Government would interfere in their behalf for their protection and rights, the war parties were temporarily restrained, and they have been kept waiting to this date in expectation of the fulfillment of these promises of justice. They have asked that the murderers be punished; or, if that cannot be done, that restitution be made them, and, at least, that the property stolen from them be returned.

The attention of the Governor of Kansas has been frequently called to this subject, with the request for the return of the property, but without securing final action. The Governor has silently ignored the wrongs of the Osages in all this matter, and the property taken from them has been sold, or destroyed, or lost, being treated as plunder lawfully captured in war.

I am now informed by the agent that these Osage Indians are deeply grieved and incensed. The customary morning and evening wails of the orphans and widows are still kept up in the Osage villages, and it is with the utmost difficulty that they are daily restrained from going out in what are called "mourning parties," to assuage their grief in the blood of white men.

I do not know that any further action on the part of the Department is at all practicable; but it is due both to the records of this Bureau and the Department that these statements should be made, and that the Governor of Kansas should be again informed of the feelings of the Osages, in view of the outrages committed upon them.

It is possible, however, that if these "mourning" Osages were assured by their agent that the Department will ask of Congress, at its next session, a sum of money sufficient to satisfy them — say five thousand dollars — the agent may be able to restrain them, in the expectation of this reparation; and I respectfully request that authority may be given me to make such assurance to the agent, and to instruct him to use all means in his power, under this pledge of the Department, to prevent the Osages from taking justice into their own hands.

Very respectfully, your obedient servant,

EDWARD P. SMITH, *Commissioner.*

The Honorable Secretary of the Interior.

[COPY.]

DEPARTMENT OF THE INTERIOR, }
WASHINGTON, D. C., July 13, 1875. }

SIR: I have considered your report of the 3d inst., inviting the attention of the Department to the massacre of Osages in August last by a lawless party of Kansas citizens, led by a person named Ricker, who were subsequently ordered upon duty by orders ante-dated to cover the murders.

As suggested by you, the attention of the Governor of Kansas has been this day invited to the subject—a copy of letter to him inclosed herewith.

Authority to inform the Agent of the Osages that the Department will recommend favorable action by Congress in their behalf at the next session, is hereby granted according to your suggestion, and you will instruct the Agent to assure the Indians of the intention of the Department in the premises, and to use every effort in his power to prevent the Osages from committing any act in retaliation for the wrongs they have suffered at the hands of the citizens of Kansas.

Very respectfully, your obedient servant,

C. DELANO, *Secretary.*

The Commissioner of Indian Affairs.

EXECUTIVE DEPARTMENT, }
TOPEKA, KANSAS, July 20, 1875. }

Hon. C. Delano, Secretary of the Interior:

SIR: In the letter of the Commissioner of Indian Affairs, of date July 3d, accompanying your letter to me of the 13th inst., in reference to the conflict, in August last, between Capt. Ricker's company of militia and a band of Osage Indians, I find this sentence:

"The facts in the case are abundantly sustained by the affidavits of more than fifteen reputable citizens, who were eye-witnesses to the transaction, and on their testimony it is palpably evident that the affair was a cold-blooded murder, followed by theft and robbery."

I have the honor to request that you will cause to be forwarded to me certified copies of these affidavits, in order that I may know upon what grounds the Commissioner bases his declaration that the militia of this State has been guilty of murder and robbery.

Very respectfully, your obedient servant,

THOMAS A. OSBORN, *Governor.*

DEPARTMENT OF THE INTERIOR, }
WASHINGTON, D. C., July 31, 1875. }

SIR: For your information, and in reply to your letter of the 20th inst., I have the honor to transmit herewith a copy of a report, dated the 23d instant, from the Commissioner of Indian Affairs, to whom your communication was referred, together with copies of papers referred to by that officer, in relation to the murder of Osage Indians by citizens of Kansas.

Very respectfully, your obedient servant,

C. DELANO, *Secretary.*

Hon. Thomas A. Osborn, Governor of Kansas.

[COPY.]

DEPARTMENT OF THE INTERIOR, }
OFFICE OF INDIAN AFFAIRS, }
WASHINGTON, D. C., July 23, 1875. }

SIR: I have the honor to acknowledge the receipt, by reference from you, of a letter from Hon. Thomas A. Osborn, Governor of Kansas, dated 20th July, 1875, requesting certified copies of the affidavits referred to in the report from this office of the 3d instant, in reference to the conflict in August last between Capt. Ricker's company of militia and a band of Osage Indians.

In reply, I respectfully state that nine affidavits by "citizens" were transmitted to the Hon. Secretary of the Interior, February 24th, 1875, with report relative to this subject; and accompanying the report of F. H. Smith, J. W. Smith, and Hon. Wilson Shannon, commissioners to investigate the killing of the Osage Indians referred to, are several affidavits and copies of affidavits (some of them are made by Osage Indians, and not by "citizens") relative to the subject. These, with the report of the commission, were submitted to the Department under date of October 12, 1874. These constitute all the affidavits on the subject that have been received at this office.

The letter of Governor Osborn is herewith returned.

Very respectfully, your obedient servant,

EDWARD P. SMITH, *Commissioner.*

The Honorable Secretary of the Interior.

EXECUTIVE DEPARTMENT, }
TOPEKA, KANSAS, Sept. 11, 1875. }

Hon. C. Delano, Secretary of the Interior:

SIR: Your communication of July 13th last, covering a statement of the Commissioner of Indian Affairs, touching an alleged "outrage" perpetrated upon a band of Osage Indians by a company of Kansas Militia, in August, 1874, has been duly considered. The questions presented seem to be, first, the one of fact, having reference to the circumstances connected with the killing of the four Osage Indians; and, second, the propriety of the action of the State Government in that regard.

In the outset, I desire to call your special attention to a statement contained in the Commissioner's letter forwarded by you. He says: "The facts in the case are abundantly sustained by the affidavits of more than fifteen reputable citizens, who were eyewitnesses to the transaction, and on their testimony it is palpably evident that the affair was a cold-blooded murder, followed by theft and robbery." Immediately upon the receipt of your letter I addressed you, as you are aware, requesting copies of the affidavits referred to, and I now have the honor to acknowledge the receipt of the same from your Department.

I well knew that an extraordinary effort had been made by the Indian Bureau to obtain affidavits from people living in the vicinity where the difficulty occurred, tending to show that the Indians killed were on a peaceful expedition; yet I could not think it possible that, notwithstanding this effort, "fifteen reputable citizens" could be found in that locality who would make oath to any such state of facts as would warrant the conclusion arrived at by the Commissioner. The investigations which had been made from this office were of such a character as to render reasonably certain the circumstances surrounding the killing of these Indians. The result of these investigations is the inevitable conclusion that the Indians were off their reservation, and in the State, in violation of orders from both the civil and military authorities of the General Government, and for a hostile purpose. Hence, I say, in view of the vigilance which had been exercised by the State authorities in the effort to ascertain the facts, and the result of such effort, I knew there must be some mistake on the part of the Commissioner in this statement; and that I was not in error the affidavits forwarded by you fully prove.

There are, it is true, just fifteen affidavits from "citizens," but six of these emphatically corroborate the report of Capt. Ricker, and state that the Indians commenced the firing. The other nine affidavits differ somewhat as to the circumstances connected with the engagement, but they all utterly fail, I submit, to warrant any such statement as that made by the Commissioner of Indian Affairs. The Commissioner certainly could not have known that several "citizens" whose affidavits he has on file, and whose characters he so emphatically indorses, were, for good cause, dropped from the rolls of Capt. Ricker's company; and he must have overlooked the fact that one of the "reputable citizens" referred to by him had *two* affidavits on file in his office, in one of which he swears positively that the Indians fired first and in the other that they did not fire at all.

Now let me, in as succinct a manner as possible, review the action of the State Government in regard to this matter. In so far as I may refer to the horrors of the Indian campaign of the summer of 1874, it will be done for the single purpose of showing the condition of matters here in the State at the time of the engagement which has given rise to this controversy.

The details of last year's Indian outrages in Kansas are too sickening for contemplation, and I would now gladly avoid all reference to them, and, so far as I can with propriety, will do so. The Department of the Interior is aware of the fact that during the past year many citizens of this State, while attending to their legitimate business, were, within the boundaries of the State, brutally murdered by the savages. Several of these outrages were committed in Barbour county, in the vicinity of Medicine Lodge. As a natural result, homes were abandoned, and the people flocked to the towns in the neighborhood for protection. At Sun City, Kiowa and Medicine Lodge, stockades were built, and within these rudely-constructed defenses the citizens there congregated organized themselves into a military force, in pursuance of the laws of this State, for self-protection, and arms and ammunition were furnished them by the State Government for that purpose.

The entire southern border was regarded as in a state of war. United States troops were stationed in that locality, and patrolled from time to time the country bordering on the Indian Territory.

The Osages, who were supposed to have been concerned in some of the outrages, were on the 15th day of July at Salt Fork, twenty-five miles south of the Kansas State line, peremptorily ordered by Major Upham, in command of United States troops in that locality, to remain on their reservation, under penalty, in case of disobedience, of being treated as hostile; and messengers were at once dispatched for all who were absent to notify them thereof, and the settlers in the stockades were duly informed of the order. Thus matters stood until about the last of July, when the troops stationed in that locality were withdrawn, for the purpose of accompanying Gen. Miles on his expedition against the Cheyennes, and the few scattered settlers, then crowded together in the stockades, began to realize that they must rely upon themselves for protection from the savages.

It was while matters were in this condition that the band of Osage Indians referred to came into Barbour county, and when near Medicine Lodge encountered the militia under command of Captain Ricker. Captain R., in his report of the engagement, dated August 7, 1874 (a copy of which was duly forwarded to your Department), says:

"A few days ago forty of them made their appearance in front of the stockade at Kiowa, sixteen miles south of this point, where I have twenty-five of my men on duty, and examined the location of the same very closely. From there they moved east and north through the Cedar Hills. From what I can learn they are the same band that captured two teams from Wiggins a short time since. They set fire to and burned off all the range on their route. To satisfy myself in regard to the correctness and truth of these reports, I, with Lieut. Moseley and twenty-five men, left Medicine Lodge this morning and traveled northeast about fifteen miles, where I encountered between forty and fifty of the young braves of the Osage tribe. Six of them advanced toward us, while the balance of them formed for battle on a hill south of us. I halted my command and made signs for the forward ones to advance, which they did, coming up to us with their bows strung and arms in their hands, guns and revolvers cocked. I ordered them to give up their arms. Three of them did so, the other three refusing to understand me. I then, through Lieut. Moseley, who acted as interpreter for me, requested them to have the braves dismount and advance; but, in place of this, thinking perhaps that we could not understand them, they ordered them not to come, but to fire into my men, which was immediately done. The others then made a dash to stampede my horses. We then commenced firing on them, and had an exciting time for a few minutes."

The excitement on the border was very great, and the opinion was general that the border counties would, unless something could be done to insure them protection, become entirely depopulated. In this emergency, the command of Capt. Ricker was ordered into active service, to date from the day on which, as shown by his report, it had performed actual service in the field, to wit, August 7th.

On the 25th of August I was informed by Superintendent Hoag that he had reason to believe that the statements of Capt. Ricker, in his report of the engagement on the 7th, was incorrect; that the Indians were not in the State for hostile purposes. Capt. R. was immediately informed thereof, when he caused to be forwarded to this office six affidavits from persons who were present at the engagement, all unqualifiedly sustaining the report made by him. This seemed to leave no doubt as to the character of the engagement; yet, in view of the anxiety shown by the Indian authorities in regard to this one difficulty (the only one, by the way, in Kansas in which Indians were killed and not white men), I directed Captain J. W. Morris, of my staff, to proceed to Barbour county and make diligent inquiry as to the purposes of the Indians, and the circumstances surrounding the engagement. Capt. Morris spent several days in that section of country, in the execution of the duty intrusted to him, and his report, a copy of which is herewith forwarded, fully sustains that of Capt. Ricker. It had previously been determined that all hostile bands of

Indians found within the State should be treated as enemies at war; hence the disposal of the property captured from this band by State authority.

Still careful that there might be no room for doubt as to the facts, I directed the Adjutant General of the State, when he was ordered to sell the captured property, to make further and most careful inquiry, and if it should appear there was cause, no matter how slight, to believe that the Executive authority of the State had been misinformed or deceived, to make no sale, but hold the property subject to further orders. His conclusion, which will be found in his annual report, to which your attention was called January 16, 1875, fully sustained the report of Capt. Ricker and the six affidavits heretofore referred to, as well as the report of Capt. J. W. Morris. Such great care had been exercised by the State government in connection with this matter that it did not seem possible it could be mistaken as to the facts; and I had concluded that the Osage difficulty was a subject of the past. In this, however, I was in error, as appears from your letter of July 13. Recognizing the importance of the source from which that communication emanated, and the gravity of the accusation embraced in it, I concluded, notwithstanding my implicit faith in the correctness of the conclusions heretofore reached, to go over the whole ground once more, and to submit all the facts and circumstances to the test of an investigation more elaborate and more rigid than any that had preceded it. To this end, on the 10th day of August last I directed Captain Lewis Hanback, a gentleman accustomed to the methods of eliciting testimony, and competent to weigh it accurately, to proceed to Barbour county and "make a full and rigid investigation of the facts and circumstances attending the conflict between Capt. Ricker's company of State Militia and a band of Osage Indians, which occurred in the month of August, 1874. Reparation having been demanded of the State, on behalf of the Osage tribe, by the Department at Washington, the Governor desires, before taking final action upon said demand, that the circumstances which gave rise to it shall receive a thorough and impartial investigation," &c. (See this order copied in full in Capt. Hanback's report.)

This report, which is quite full, embraces the sworn testimony of some fifteen witnesses, among whom I recognize the principal

merchant at Medicine Lodge, the Probate Judge, Register of
Deeds, County Clerk, County Attorney, Clerk of the District
Court, Sheriff and other prominent citizens of Barbour county,
and also includes the testimony of four persons who were present
at the engagement on the 7th of August. The scope of his
investigation was quite broad, covering not only the circumstances of the Indian fight, but also the character of this band of
Indians, their purposes in coming into that section, the state of
public sentiment in the community at the time and the circumstances connected with the killing of several white men in that
neighborhood a short time previously, and the Indians by whom
such outrages were perpetrated. I am confident that a careful
examination of this report will convince you that the State Government was correct in its conclusions in regard to this band of
Indians. The testimony is voluminous, and I will not refer to it
in detail; but I cannot forbear calling your attention to the
statements of several witnesses touching the identity of the Indians who had committed the several murders in Barbour county,
in the month of July. This testimony renders almost unmistak-
able the conclusion of the Adjutant General of the State, to the
effect that these outrages were committed by Osages.

The question of fact may properly rest here. There are, however, a few other considerations to be mentioned. It seems to me
that the public safety requires that Indians who have reservations
should be compelled to stay upon them (except in cases of great
emergency), at the risk of being killed if they stray from them.
People living upon the frontier, exposed to Indian depredations,
or who have suffered from them, cannot always be relied upon to
institute judicial investigations respecting the status of Indians
found roaming in their midst. The complete separation of the
white settlers and the Indians is the only reasonable guarantee of
safety to either. This policy is, practically, the policy of your
Department, and it ought to be rigidly enforced. I have before
me a press dispatch, dated Washington, December 31, 1874, to
the following effect:

"The Bureau of Indian Affairs has issued a circular letter to superintend-
ents and agents of Indian departments, instructing them to notify the several
bands or tribes of Indians under their supervision that they must confine
themselves wholly within the limits of their respective reservations; that
under no pretext must they leave without a permit in writing." . . . . .
"Whenever it shall be deemed either necessary or judicious to grant a

permit, application should be made before its issuance to the commanding
officer of the nearest military force, who will furnish a sufficient guard to
accompany and remain with the Indians as long as they remain in a white
settlement, and those who may require their passes through such settlements
must be as expeditious as possible. Indians are to be warned that without
the protection thus guaranteed them by written permit and military guard,
they are liable to be looked upon and treated as hostile bands."

The reservation of the Osages is outside of Kansas, and they
have no business in the State, certainly not unless under the
conditions prescribed by the Indian Bureau. The particular
band of Osages with whom the difficulty occurred in Barbour
county was in Kansas in violation of positive orders from the
civil and military officers of the Government, and in defiance of
orders from Lieut. Smith, of the State Militia, stationed at Kiowa,
to return to their reservation. (See testimony of Lieut. Smith,
accompanying Capt. Hanback's report.) Hence it will be seen
that the State Government has not only vindicated its own
policy, but it has also assisted in enforcing that of the General
Government.

While these Indians remain on their side of the State line,
they need apprehend no interference from our citizens; but it is
high time that they understood that they can trespass upon the
State only at their peril.

The demand made by the Commissioner of Indian Affairs,
and sanctioned by you, that the State should compensate the
Osages for the ponies and property captured in this Barbour
county conflict, prompts me to urge that Kansas would be very
glad to reach a complete adjustment of all pending Indian claims;
and while I never can admit that she ought to pay a single dollar on this particular account, still, in order to facilitate a settlement, I assume the authority to say that the allowance in full of
this demand would not be grudged by the State, in case it might
be regarded as a partial offset to the very considerable amount
due from the General Government, or the Indian tribes which
are under its control, on account of losses suffered from the
depredations of such tribes.

I need not remind you that it is a paramount duty of the Government to protect its citizens, especially from the predatory incursions of these Indian tribes over which it professes to exercise
a strict supervision. I cannot but recognize the difficulty of the
task, and therefore I insist that credit, rather than blame, is due

to the local authorities for their aid in a work to which the General Government alone seemed to be inadequate.

During its brief history, this State has expended from its treasury more than $300,000 in the defense of the people against Indian hostilities, nearly $40,000 of which was expended in the campaign of last year. Every dollar of this amount should be repaid by the United States, and I appeal to you as the head of the Department having charge of Indian affairs, to recommend that Congress make provision for this act of justice.

Besides, citizens of this State have claims to a very considerable amount against numerous Indian tribes for losses and damages sustained by reason of their depredations. A large proportion of these claims have been properly examined and audited by commissioners empowered by act of the Legislature, and the results submitted to Congress. The commission which sat in 1872 allowed claims of this character to the amount of $119,-807.66, of which I find chargeable to the Osages the sum of $18,290.96. These are legitimate claims for property of peaceful citizens captured or destroyed by thieving Indians. They should be satisfied from the annuity fund set apart for these Indians.

This Osage difficulty has been the occasion of much labor and of an exceedingly voluminous correspondence on the part of this department. In perfect good faith, the State Government has sought to ascertain all the facts. In view of these facts, I am bound to maintain that the action of the militia in Barbour county was both justifiable and proper, and consequently that the demand upon the State for "reparation" is without warrant. This conclusion is based upon the several investigations detailed in the foregoing. I can conceive of no testimony that would be likely to modify it, and therefore I respectfully request that it may be regarded as the final determination of the State Government.

I have the honor to be, sir, very respectfully,

Your obedient servant,

THOS. A. OSBORN, *Governor.*

REPORT OF CAPTAIN J. W. MORRIS.

HUTCHINSON, KANSAS, August 17, 1874.

To Col. C. A. Morris, Adjutant General, Topeka, Kansas:

SIR: I have the honor to report that in accordance with instructions I have investigated the encounter between the State Militia and a band of Osage Indians, in Barbour county, Kansas, on the 7th day of August, 1874, and find the following to be the facts: On or about the 1st day of August, 1874, a war party of between forty and fifty mounted Osages, consisting mostly of young men in full war paint, made their appearance close to the stockade at Kiowa, in Barbour county, and after an apparently careful survey of the stockade and surroundings, they departed in a southeasterly direction, and for several days following small parties of Indians were seen in different parts of the county, capturing horses and causing great uneasiness and alarm among the settlers, resulting in a general stampede and the congregating of the people of the county in the stockades at Sun City, Medicine Lodge and Kiowa.

On the 5th of August a company of United States Cavalry from Fort Dodge, on a scouting expedition west of Comanche county, struck a fresh trail of fifteen mounted Indians, leading a little north of west. The cavalry gave immediate pursuit, and the Indians, discovering they were being followed, turned their course through Comanche county, and on the 6th of August were discovered in Barbour county, near Medicine Lodge, where the cavalry were so close upon them that the Indians scattered into small parties of two and three each, and their trails were entirely lost. The soldiers then gave up the pursuit and turned back towards Fort Dodge.

On the evening of the same day a scout from Kiowa, when about twelve miles northeast of Medicine Lodge, saw several small parties of Indians making their way rapidly towards a fixed point. He followed and soon came upon a large camp of Indians which, upon closer inspection, he thought to be the force that appeared before the stockade at Kiowa on the first instant, which he reported the same night to Capt. Ricker, at Medicine Lodge.

On the following morning, August 7th, Capt. Ricker, with a detachment of twenty-three mounted men of his company, left Medicine Lodge, going in the direction where the scout had discovered the Indians the day before, and when about fifteen miles out he discovered their camp. Wishing to ascertain whether the Indians were hostile or friendly, Capt. Ricker marched his command into a ravine close to their camp, and when nearly opposite he rode out alone upon the high ground in full view of and within one hundred and fifty yards of the Indians, who proved to be a party of about forty-five young Osage braves. As soon as Capt. Ricker was discovered, eight or ten of the Indians mounted their ponies and came towards him with hostile demonstrations, they having their bows strung and arrows in their hands; also guns and revolvers cocked. When quite close to Capt. Ricker, the Indians saw the company of militia, which now dashed up out of the ravine, and Capt. Ricker, through an interpreter, demanded of them in the Osage language to surrender and deliver up their arms, which four of them were in the act of doing when their chief, Capt. Broke-arm's son, in the Osage language called upon the main body (who were now mounted and in line) to fire on the militia, which they promptly did, at the same time making a dash towards Capt. Ricker's company. The fire of the Indians was promptly returned by the militia, and the Osages were completely routed, leaving four of their dead on the field, one of which was the son of Broke-arm, the chief who ordered the attack. The Indians were only pursued a short distance, as Capt. Ricker was apprehensive of an additional force of Osages in the vicinity. The militia captured a large number of ponies and mules, with which they returned to Medicine Lodge the same day.

Very respectfully, your obedient servant,

J. W. MORRIS,
Captain, and Aid-de-Camp.

[For the conclusions of Adjutant General C. A. Morris, touching this subject, see his annual report for 1874.]

REPORT OF CAPTAIN LEWIS HANBACK.

TOPEKA, KANSAS, August 24, 1875.

Major H. T. Beman, Asst. Adjutant General:

SIR: I have the honor to report, that on the 10th day of August, 1875, I received the following orders from the Governor and Commander-in-Chief:

STATE OF KANSAS, OFFICE OF ADJUTANT GENERAL,
TOPEKA, August 10, 1875.

SPECIAL ORDERS No. 18.]

To Captain Lewis Hanback, Special Aid-de-Camp:

SIR: You are hereby instructed to make a full and rigid investigation of the facts and circumstances attending the conflict between Captain Ricker's company of State militia and a band of Osage Indians, which occurred in Barbour county, Kansas, in the month of August, 1874.

You will receive, herewith, for your information, communications from the Secretary of the Interior and the Commissioner of Indian Affairs, together with accompanying affidavits, seeking to maintain that in the conflict above mentioned, Capt. Ricker and his command made an attack without provocation upon peaceful Indians, and were guilty of the murder of four of said Indians, and of the unlawful taking of ponies and other property belonging to said band.

Reparation having been demanded of the State, on behalf of the Osage tribe, by the Department at Washington, the Governor desires before taking final action upon said demand, that the circumstances which gave rise to it shall receive a thorough and impartial investigation. To this end, you will, without delay, proceed to Barbour county, and make strict inquiry as to the affair in question, with all its surroundings.

You will consult with as many as practicable of those who were members of said militia company at the time of the conflict in question, as well as other persons having knowledge of the circumstances; and will cause the testimony taken to be reduced to writing, and duly verified. Having made your investigation as thorough as possible under the circumstances, you will return to this city and report the results thereof, in writing, to the Governor, together with the testimony taken.

By order of the Governor.   H. T. BEMAN,
Assistant Adjutant General.

In obedience to the above orders, I left Topeka on the afternoon of the 10th inst., taking the A., T. & Santa Fe Railway to Hutchinson, and by stage to the town of Medicine Lodge, the county seat of Barbour county, where I arrived on the evening of the 11th.

Thursday and Friday were occupied in meeting citizens of the county, and explaining to them my mission and its object. On Friday evening, a meeting of the citizens of the town and surrounding country was held at the school-house, at which there was a fair attendance. I explained to the meeting the object of my visit, and read to them all of the correspondence which had passed between the Executive Department of the State and the Secretary of the Interior and the Commissioner of Indian Affairs, together with the report of a commission consisting of Mahlon Stubbs, —— Finney, and L. B. Kellogg, who had been appointed by Agent I. T. Gibson of the Osages, to investigate the alleged killing of four Osage Indians on the 7th of August, 1874, by a portion of the Kansas militia under command of Capt. C. M. Ricker. I also read to the meeting the separate report of Mahlon Stubbs (who is Agent of the Kansas tribe of Indians), made by request of Special Commissioner Smith, of the Indian Department, to the President's Peace Commission.

In doing this, I was actuated by a desire to place the whole matter in as succinct and clear a light as possible before the citizens of Barbour county, rendering thereby compliance with the orders under which I was acting.

I explained to the meeting that I was among them solely for the purpose of arriving at the true state of the facts connected with the Indian troubles of 1874, and to this end the hearty co-operation of the citizens was requested. I am happy to be able to report that in all the investigation which subsequently followed, I met with but little opposition, if any; and I avail myself of this opportunity to express my thanks for the courteous assistance extended to me by the citizens of the county with whom it was my good fortune to meet.

From Saturday until Wednesday, I was engaged in taking testimony, and in visiting different portions of the county and meeting citizens. I respectfully submit the accompanying testimony, taken in the form of interrogatories, as the result of my labors. In every case, before I commenced taking the testimony of a witness, I explained to him that I desired a full statement of the facts as he knew them, either from personal observation, or from information in which he had an implicit reliance, and as near as

3

possible the testimony of each witness was taken down in his or her own language.

Barbour county was originally a part of the Indian reservation belonging to the Osages. It is one of the largest counties in the State; is well supplied with running streams, and heavy crops of buffalo grass. Its winters are generally mild, and these, with the other fact that it is and has been the resort of all kinds of large game, made it a favorite hunting ground for the Osages. That tribe held almost undisputed sway over it, even after its cession, until within the past four years, when settlements of white men began to be formed, and so rapidly as to speedily dispute the sway theretofore exercised over it. The result was, that game became less abundant, and rendered hunting more difficult and arduous. Traveling bands of Osages and other tribes were frequently found within the limits of the county. There could be but one result brought about by such a state of things. The settlements grew, and the Indians became more and more jealous of the encroachment of the whites. Occasionally news would be received of some settler being killed and scalped, or of horses and stock stolen and run off. Prominent among the citizens killed was John Moseley, who for a number of years had been one of the advanced pioneers of the State. In the winter of 1873 he was attacked in his house on Medicine Lodge creek, by a band of Osages, and, after several hours' fighting, was killed. C. C. Leonard and another settler was with him at the time. After he was killed, the Indians retreated, driving off some stock. I have made arrangements to have the testimony of Leonard taken, and forwarded to your office.

In this way matters continued until the winter of 1874. There had been no general uprising of the Indians, such as would cause a state of uneasiness. While it was known that there was bad blood among the various tribes, and especially the Osages, yet there was a comparative feeling of safety in existence among the settlers. But during the winter and spring of 1874, a different state of facts arose. Information was brought in by hunters to Medicine Lodge, that a general uprising among the Indians was being by them contemplated and discussed. This news was entitled to credence. It came from men whose education in such matters was complete, and whose judgment was relied upon; who had heard the talk, and noted the preparations being made in the various lodges and camps of the Cheyennes, Osages, Arapahoes and Kiowas. The cause of additional belief in the minds of the hunters, was that they noticed that the Indians used only bows and arrows for killing their game, saving their ammunition; and also that they were anxious to barter for ammunition. And, in addition to this, the Indians told them that when the grass grew the white men would lose their hair. (See testimony of D. E. Sheldon.)

It appears from the testimony taken by me, and also from information which I received, that all of these circumstances, facts and rumors, were transmitted to the settlers, and were by them understood. So that when spring came and the grass began to grow, there was a vigilant outlook kept up for apprehended troubles; but as the season advanced and no depredations had been committed, a feeling of security settled upon the citizens, and all thought of harm from Indian sources dwindled into insignificance. Thus matters continued until the 16th of June, 1874. But prior to that time, and as early as the 9th of April, 1874, a party of Cheyennes, of Little Robe's band, stole a lot of stock near Sun City, in Barbour county, and succeeded in getting away with the greater part of it. Other acts of a similar nature were committed along the frontier, and it was noticed that the Indians of the various tribes were sullen, and in some cases insolent. Yet no overt act was committed until the 16th of June, when the town of Kiowa was attacked, and after a large number of shots had been fired into the houses, the Indians withdrew, taking with them four horses. From subsequent developments, it appears that this party, numbering eleven, camped that night on Mule creek, and next day passed unobserved, except by a young man named Dwinnell, but a short distance south of Medicine Lodge.

On the morning of the 17th, two men, named respectively Martin and Kennedy, passed through Medicine Lodge in their wagons, on their way to the Cedar Hills for rails. Two days afterward, they were found in a cedar canyon, six miles southwest of town, dead and scalped; their horses were missing. On the 17th, about 11 o'clock in the forenoon, Isaac Keim, while driving along the road leading to his claim, on Little Mule creek (and about two miles from where Martin and Kennedy were killed), was ambushed, killed and scalped, and his horses

taken. All these depredations and murders were undoubtedly
committed by the same party which had attacked Kiowa the
day before, as a clear trail was made from the canyon to where
Keim was killed. Attention is here called to the testimony of
Mrs. Sarah Garlinghouse, who, with her two children, were in
their house, not over two hundred yards from the place of
Keim's murder. Mrs. Garlinghouse is a woman of more than
ordinary sense. Nearly her whole life has been passed on the
frontier, in the midst of and in close proximity to the Cheyennes,
Arapahoes, Osages and Kiowas. Her father is a noted pioneer
and plainsman, and both by education and observation she is
well qualified to express an opinion as to what tribe the Indians
who killed Keim belonged to. In addition to this, and as add-
ing to the weight of her testimony, she is a woman of irreproach-
able character, enjoying, to the fullest extent, the confidence and
respect of all who know her. I know this to be a fact, because
I took pains to ascertain what those who knew her thought of
her, and what reliance was to be placed upon her judgment; to all
my inquiries there was but one response: that she knew what she
was talking about, being as well versed in Indian matters—their
habits and dress—as any person in the county. Her testimony
is of the greatest importance, being, as she was, the only eye-
witness of the horrible deed. She swears she thought at the
time they were Osages, and her description of the way they
wore their hair (cut short, while all the other tribes heretofore
mentioned wear their hair long), the style of their dress, their
manner, all indicate that she was correct in her judgment, and
that the murderers of Martin, Kennedy and Keim were members of the Osage tribe.

The news of the murders of these peaceable and unoffending
citizens was soon transmitted to all the settlers in the county. A
reign of terror ensued. Homes were deserted at once, and the
towns were soon crowded with the settlers, gathered together for
mutual protection. Active measures were resorted to for the public defense. Assistance was sought from the State and furnished as
rapidly as possible. A continued state of alarm existed. It was
deemed utterly unsafe to travel beyond the limits of the towns,
which were all stockaded, except in force. Authority being
given, C. M. Ricker enrolled a company of about sixty men, the
greater part of whom were armed and mounted. Frequent

scouts were made. Pickets were posted at night, and to all in-tents and purposes a state of war existed. All Indians found within the limits of the county were *prima facie* deemed enemies, and none were considered more so than the Osages. Treacherous and cowardly as they are, it was believed that they only awaited a safe opportunity for murder and robbery. Nor were these fears based on groundless conjecture, for it appears that during these times Agent I. T. Gibson arrived at Medicine Lodge and endeavored to get an escort and conveyance to go with him in search of a part of Black Dog's band of Osages, which he (Gib-son) said was somewhere in that portion of the country off their reservation, and against his advice and consent, and he feared they would join the Cheyennes and other Indians on the war-path. (See Dr. T. W. Davis's testimony.) All of the statements of Gibson were talked of and canvassed by the inhabitants of Medicine Lodge, and afforded additional food to their fears.

In the fore part of July Charles C. Bond, by profession a phy-sician, while early one morning on his way to Sun City, was met by a party of Osages, four in number, and narrowly escaped with his life, seven shots being fired at him. Although pursued by a force of militia then stationed at Lake City, the Indians escaped, taking with them several horses belonging to Abraham Winnie and William Carl. On their trail and during their pursuit was found a woman's scalp which had been but recently taken, show-ing that the party had been on the war-path.

Dr. Bond, who makes an affidavit of the above facts, is a worthy and an intelligent man, and one of a very few who had remained outside of the stockades, as he believed there was no danger from Indians. It is needless to say that he changed his opinion in a very few moments after his narrow escape. I re-spectfully direct attention to his statement.

At about this same time two men who lived in Sumner county but were in Barbour county after a load of cedar, were return-ing home, when they were overtaken by a party of Indians (Osages) and their teams taken from them. Personally they were not molested, but they reported the Indians insolent, and deemed it a providential act that their lives were not taken. In this connection I might remark that both Winnie and Carl are now prosecuting their claims against the Osages for taking their property, and that their claim has been recognized in part

by Agent Gibson, additional proof being only required to perfect
their claim.

Thus matters continued until the early part of August, 1874,
when about the 4th or 5th a party of Osages appeared near the
town of Kiowa. The band numbered over thirty warriors, and
was under the command of the Indian who has heretofore been
referred to as having but one eye. They were visited by Lieut.
Eli Smith, then in command of a portion of Ricker's company
stationed at that place. By his testimony, which is herewith
submitted, together with the testimony of Levi Davis, it appeared
they claimed to be a buffalo hunting party. Lieut. Smith testifies that he ordered them to return to their reservation, which
they failed and refused to do. The testimony of Lieut. Smith, in the
light of subsequent events, is important, and justifies the reasonable
conclusion which he arrives at, that hunting buffalo was only a
pretext; and as reasons for his conclusion he says they kept as
nearly as possible their arms concealed. They would not talk
English. One of the Indians was painted, his horse was painted,
he was armed with a shield, and he was in every respect gotten
up in war style. Added to this, he was insolent in his manner.
Smith tried to talk with the Indian with one eye, who it was
known could talk English, but he paid no attention to him
(Lieut. Smith), pretending he could not understand.

As bearing upon the mission of these Indians, reference is had
to the conversation which Lieut. Smith subsequently had with
Mahlon Stubbs, agent for the Kansas Indians, and whose admis-
sions and statements are from the very nature of things important,
it being presumable that Stubbs would make no statements of
the kind referred to unless he was certain of their absolute truth.
Yet Stubbs states to Smith, in the presence of John Moseley, in
front of the residence of Judge Updegraff, at Medicine Lodge,
that this same party was a mourning band, which is in reality a
war party. The facts in the case are that these Indians were
warned not to remain, and were ordered to return to their reservation. Their presence in the county and their failure to obey
the order of Lieut. Smith was by that officer on the next day
communicated by him in person to Capt. Ricker.

I now come to the important part of the mission upon which I
was sent, to wit: to make careful inquiry into the facts of the
engagement of August 7th, with the Osages, in which four Osages

were killed. The testimony of Iliff, Lampton, Van Slyke and Garlinghouse may be relied upon. Their testimony was taken separately, and neither knew what the others had testified to. Added to this, they are all men of respectability.

On the evening of the 6th of August, 1874, about nine o'clock, the town of Medicine Lodge was suddenly thrown into a state of excitement, caused by the arrival of S. J. Shepler and his son Frank, who brought with them information to the effect that a party of Osage Indians were in camp about fifteen miles northeast from town. Shepler and son were both laboring under excitement, and Shepler stated to Friedley that he believed he would have been scalped if he had had a horse or mule instead of an ox team. He (Shepler) urged Ricker to take his men out and investigate the cause of the Indians being off their reservation.

Orders were therefore at once issued for rations to be prepared for twenty-five men, officers included.

On the morning of the 7th the command marched in the direction indicated by Shepler. At noon halted for a short time and then moved on. About 1 o'clock Ricker's attention was called by Lampton and others to what they thought was a camp. He thought it was only some logs, and started forward (the command being halted) to reconnoiter. In a very short time he was seen returning on the run, swinging his hat; whereupon the command moved forward to the top of the ridge immediately in front, formed in line, and then moved a short distance, when one Indian, mounted and advancing, was discovered, being near our line. He was forced to come in, and was quickly followed by others, who, as they came in, were disarmed or nearly so. By this time our line had moved to a point within sight of the Indian camp, and for the first time saw the whole Indian force, drawn up in line of battle, some three hundred yards distant. The Indians who had been captured were placed on the right flank of our line, and six men had been dismounted for the purpose of a guard. The rest of the command remained mounted, and were in full view of the Indians in line. The captured Indians were, therefore, in no danger from any attack which their comrades might make. Matters remained in this state but a moment, when Capt. Ricker ordered the Indian who claimed to be chief to order those remaining in line to come up. The Indian did

halloo to them in the Osage language, when Lieut. Moseley, who
was on his horse near by, and who thoroughly understands the
Osage language, sprang towards him and told him that if he told
the Indians again to fire on our line he would blow his brains
out, or in language to that effect. I was unable to obtain the
testimony of Lieut. Moseley, who is now in Texas, but have made
arrangements to have it taken as soon as he returns. At once
the captured Indians gave a yell, and commenced a most desperate and determined effort to escape. Iliff was beaten over the
head, and eventually knocked to his knees; Van Slyke was run
over; commotion was noticed in the main line; there was every indication that a battle had been begun. Garlinghouse's
testimony on this point is important. He has been in a number
of Indian fights, and he testifies that the action of the Indians
on the 7th was the same as he had always observed under similar
circumstances, and that at the time he "thought they had come
out to give us a stand-off." Be this as it may, whether the
Indians meant peace or war there was no time to consider. The
two lines were apparently in hostile. array, prisoners captured
were escaping, when our line, justified by every precept of
sense and safety, opened fire on the Indians in line and
those escaping. Van Slyke says the whole affair did not last
more than two minutes. The result was that four Indians were
killed. The retreating line was followed some three miles, no
shots being fired owing to the great distance which intervened.

Up to this time it was not known that the Indians had so
large a number of horses, ponies, etc., concealed in the brush,
but when the command returned to the Indian camp, it was ascertained that over fifty head of stock had been discovered,
which was taken possession of, brought to Medicine Lodge, an
inventory thereof taken, and forwarded in due time to the Adjutant General of the State. Afterwards, this stock was taken
possession of by the State, as being captured in war. All the
testimony bearing upon the subject shows that the command,
when it returned to Medicine Lodge, was received with demonstrations of joy.

Such, in brief, is a statement of the facts of the engagement of
August 7th, as will be seen by a reference to the testimony herewith submitted. And upon the testimony, which contains an

incontrovertible statement of facts, I beg leave to submit the following conclusions:

I submit that from June 17 to the latter part of September, there was an actual state of Indian war existing in Barbour county; that the country outside of the stockade towns was given up, and was a common battle-ground; that it was wholly unsafe for white men to travel outside of the towns, unless in bodies and properly armed; that there were armed bands of Indians scouting through the country for the purpose of robbery and murder; that a part of these bands were made up of Osages; that there was a necessity, every day more apparent, which led the settlers to arm and organize themselves into military bodies for the purpose of mutual protection; and that they were so organized solely for protection, and not for the purpose (as has been charged in high places) of murder and theft. From all I could see and hear, both from conversation with the settlers who formed Ricker's company and those who did not, I bear willing testimony that they are to all appearances peaceful and law-abiding citizens. They indignantly scout the idea, sought by certain parties to be maintained, that they were organized for any other than a purely legitimate purpose. It was only by organization that the horrors of an Indian war could be averted. They were near three hundred miles from the seat of government; separated from civilization by many miles of almost trackless prairies, and in the immediate vicinity of powerful tribes of Indians, known to be hostile whenever the opportunity offered; added to this, robberies had been committed, and peaceful, unoffending citizens, their neighbors and friends, brutally murdered. Organization was, therefore, for protection from like horrors, an imminent necessity. A careful examination of all the facts will lead to but one conclusion: that the Indians attacked on the 7th of August were a war party. They were a party of Black Dog's band, who, according to Agent Gibson, had left their reservation against his advice and consent; they were declared by Stubbs (Agent of the Kansas Indians) to be a mourning party; they were undoubtedly a part of the same band which committed outrages of murder and robbery in Ford, Barbour and Comanche counties, prior to the 7th. At Kiowa they were met by Lieut. Smith, and ordered back to their reservation, which order they refused to obey. While there they were insolent; one of their number was in full war costume; their chief, the Indian with one eye, refused to talk English; in fact, all the surroundings of the party were those of a hostile character. Despite the testimony of some of the Indians, there was no party of women or children with them.

That this was a war party, is abundantly shown by the action of the Indians on the 7th. At first, Ricker alone was seen; pursuit was immediately commenced after him. If for the purpose of peace, was it necessary that these Indians should have advanced with bows drawn and arrows in hand? Was it necessary that a peaceful party should be decked in war costumes, and themselves and horses daubed in war paints? or was it necessary for a peaceful party to form in line of battle, either to give or receive an attack? Added to this, there is no doubt in my mind but that Lieut. Moseley interpreted the language of the Indian who acted as chief, when he directed the Indians in line to fire on our troops, and that our line understood from Moseley, as well as the action of the Indians, that such directions had been given. The Indians knew the troubled state of affairs as they then existed, and if only on a mission of peace, they were well enough versed in such matters to have made known the cause of their presence. Failing to avail themselves of the rights accorded to peaceful Indians, it was right that they should be treated as enemies, and I entertain no doubt that every man in Ricker's command, from captain to the last private, entertained but one belief on that day: that they had confronted a war party of Osages. Those who testify say so, and the circumstances justify the conclusions in the fullest measure.

The attempt made by the Indian authorities to fasten the charge of murder and robbery on the whites, is wholly and utterly without foundation. It arises either from a misconception of the facts, or a willful desire to malign and misrepresent. As I cannot believe it is the latter, it must be the former, and in this I am sustained. I charge that the statement of Mahlon Stubbs to the President's Peace Commission is but the product of his imagination, and in every important particular is wholly and utterly false; and in the same category may be placed the statement of the Osage Indians. If proof was required to show the animus which governed the efforts of Gibson and Hoag to obtain testimony which should reflect on the whites and exonerate the Indians, it may be found in the action of Rankin, who was sent down by Enoch Hoag to Medicine Lodge, in January last. Instead of going there for the truth in an open, manly way, he went in the character of a spy and detective. When he arrived at Hutchinson, he presented to Chas. C. Collins a letter of introduction, and asked for free transportation to Medicine Lodge, over the stage route of which Collins is owner. He stated he was going there to look up a suitable sheep claim, with a view of making a settlement. When he arrived at Medicine Lodge, he did not make his business known; he kept aloof from the inhabitants. He sent for those citizens who were known to be disaffected with the state of affairs (see testimony of Van Slyke), and having secured all he could he left, without locating his sheep claim. His action is not the course which a man honestly seeking the truth would pursue.

I have endeavored, in this hastily-drawn report, to give a correct history of the Indian troubles in Barbour county, such as will stand the test of testimony, no matter how elaborately taken.

All of which is respectfully submitted.

LEWIS HANBACK,
Captain, and Special Aid-de-Camp.

EVIDENCE TAKEN BY CAPT. LEWIS HANBACK.

TESTIMONY OF D. E. SHELDON

Interrogatory 1: What is your name, place of residence, and occupation?

Answer: My name is D. E. Sheldon; residence, Medicine Lodge, Barbour county, Kansas; occupation, merchant. I have resided in Barbour county something over two years.

Int. 2: Were you a resident of Barbour county, Kansas, in the spring and summer of 1874? and if so, state what you know of the origin of the Indian troubles of that year; and in this connection state the condition of the settlers relative to their being in a continued state of alarm during that time.

Ans.: I was a resident of Barbour county during that time. Through the winter and spring we had heard, through the hunters that came into Medicine Lodge to trade, and by hunters residing in our midst, that they believed that the various tribes along the border were intending to go on the war-path in the spring. The cause of their believing it was that the Indians told them, in their various lodges and camps, that that was their intention; also by making gestures that when the grass grew, they (the white men) would lose their hair; furthermore, that they noticed that the Indians did all their killing with bows and arrows, saving their ammunition, and were anxious to trade for ammunition whenever they had a chance. It was said that the Cheyennes, Arapahoes, Comanches and Osages were expected to unite. These tribes were expected to hold a council of war to decide whether they would join in battle against the whites in the spring. I was informed such a council was held. In the latter part of the winter, two Indians, one of whom was a delegate or commissioner (according to his representations) to this council, stopped at my store. He said there was a council to be held in about two weeks at the mouth of Medicine Lodge, for the purpose of consulting as to whether the above tribes should join against the whites or not. I was afterwards informed by Agent Gibson, of the Osages, that he sent a number of Osages to that council for the purpose of keeping peace, but that the Osage delegates were divided at the council, a part being for war and a part for peace. I had this conversation with him on the road between Medicine Lodge and Caldwell. All of this information was communicated to the settlers in Barbour county, and thoroughly canvassed and understood; and it was for these reasons that it was generally believed that we were liable to be massacred at any time by the before-mentioned tribes. However, up to June 17, 1874, there had been no depredations committed near Medicine Lodge, but on the 17th of June, 1874, in the afternoon, several families came into town in great terror, stating that there had been a man by the name of Keim murdered by Indians on Cedar creek, about six miles from here. In a short time four young men went out to investigate the matter, and returned in the evening with the body of said Keim. His horses were gone, his harness cut to pieces, and groceries and such things as he had in the wagon were scattered over the ground. One Mrs. Martin Garlinghouse was alone at the time with her children but a few hundred yards from the place of the murder. Her house was out of view from the place where Keim was killed, by some trees and brush, but she heard the firing, ran out of the house to where she could see, saw the Indians committing their hellish work, and then saw them leaving in great speed. On the morning of Keim's murder, two men by the name of Martin and Kennedy passed through this place on their way to the hills to get rails to fence their corn field. On the morning of the 18th, as these men had not passed through here on their way to their homes, the people became alarmed for their safety and went out in search of them. Searched that day, and returned without any success. On the morning of the 19th Mrs. Martin came to town from some three miles, bringing her child with her. She was in delicate health. She was in great alarm in consequence of her husband not returning the night before, as he told her he would be home at noon of the 17th. She did not know that Keim had been killed by the Indians until she arrived in town, and you can imagine the state of her feelings. Search was renewed on the morning of the 19th, with success. The bodies were found, in a state of decomposition. Martin was chopping, as it appears, under a high bluff of some thirty or forty feet above him and nearly perpendicular. It appears that they had slipped up behind him as he was chopping (standing upon a log), and shot him, one ball passing through his back and one through the back of his hand, cutting the ax-handle, showing that he was chopping at the time, with his hand raised. Kennedy, it seems, ran some distance around a clump of brush, but it appears there were Indians on the opposite side of the canyon, when he was shot in plain view, two balls entering his head. The surroundings showed that the killing was done by volleys. They were both scalped. There were two horses and one two-year-old colt, all taken. The wagon and harness were left standing. It was plain to see where they entered the canyon after the killing and where they went out with the two horses and colt afterwards. The indications showed that there were about eleven Indians in the party of Indians. There were no boot tracks—all moccasin tracks. On the 15th or 16th of June the town of Kiowa was attacked by a party of Indians. A number of shots were fired into the houses, and four horses were stolen. The Indians then retreated, and that night camped on Mule creek. The next morning they marched to Medicine Lodge creek, and during the forenoon were seen by a young man named Orris Dwinell, traveling about one mile from his house. He supposed they were hunters or soldiers, and paid no attention to them. This was the same party which killed Martin, Kennedy and Keim. They passed up the creek in full sight of the town of Medicine Lodge, (but were not noticed,) over to the canyon where Martin and Kennedy were chopping, and undoubtedly heard the chopping. After disposing of them (Martin and Kennedy), the trail showed that they crossed over the divide toward Cedar creek, when they came across Keim in the road, surrounded and killed him. In consequence of these depredations, the whole country was thrown into a state of war. The citizens outside of the towns left their homes, and sought safety in the towns. Medicine Lodge was inclosed with a stockade, and every means were taken for protection. In fact, the country outside of the towns was given up, and became a common battle-ground between the whites and Indians. Each point where the people were gathered was stockaded, and was guarded by armed men. Scouts were thrown out during the day and pickets at night, the same as done in a state of war. On the evening of the 6th of August, Mr. S. J. Shepler came in under a state of excitement, stating that there was a body of Indians some sixteen miles northeast of here, encamped, and he thought it advisable that the company, which was termed militia, under command of Capt. Ricker, should go out and investigate them. In consequence, next morning there were about twenty-five men, mounted, marched out under command of Capt. Ricker, when the Indians were discovered and a skirmish took place. In the evening they returned with some fifty or more ponies, colts and mules, and reported they had killed four Indians and chased the balance some three or four miles. The stock were cared for until orders were received from the Governor of the State to hold the same until further orders. The people generally supposed, at the time the company went to investigate the cause of the Indians being within the border of the State and so near us, that they were hostile, and great joy was manifested throughout the county, and especially at Medicine Lodge, that the camp had been routed, as they deemed that their safety depended upon it, and it was generally considered an act of war and not of murder or robbery. Immediately after the captured property was brought to Medicine Lodge, an inventory was taken of it and a return thereof was made to the Governor of the State.

Int. 3: State if you was in the town of Medicine Lodge at the time Mahlon Stubbs, —— Finney, and L. B. Kellogg were here as a commission to investigate the killing of the Osages on the 7th of August.

Ans.: Yes.

Int. 4: State if you have heard read the report of Mahlon Stubbs to the President's Peace Commission, and also the report of the Commissioners to I. T. Gibson, Indian Agent for the Osages, read.

Ans.: I have.

Int. 5: Do you consider their report correct? and if not, state your reasons.

Ans.: I do not think it is correct, for the reason that I saw no unusual demonstrations of the people of the place when they first arrived, nor at any time thereafter, that would lead them to feel that they would incur any danger for the free expression of their opinions in favor of the Indians, or any subject connected with their mission. Furthermore, I don't believe that any little girl had any Osage scalp, for we professed then, and do now, to be civilized people, and not barbarians. Instead of the Commissioners appearing to be afraid, they walked about the town like any other citizens, and freely expressed their opinions; and to my certain knowledge, they were courteously treated in every respect. The militia company under command of Capt. Ricker was formed for mutual protection from savage Indians; it was formed of citizens of the town and country, and was composed of law-abiding and peaceable citizens, and not murderers and thieves. They were armed and equipped to protect themselves and families, and the Commissioners were in every respect as safe and as free from insult as they would have been in their own homes.   D. E. SHELDON.

STATE OF KANSAS, BARBOUR COUNTY, ss.

D. E. Sheldon, being duly sworn, says the statements above made by him are true in substance and in fact, as he verily believes.   D. E. SHELDON.

Subscribed and sworn to before me, this 14th day of August, A. D. 1875.   D. VAN SLYKE,

[SEAL.]   *County Clerk, Barbour County, Kansas.*

STATEMENT OF REUBEN LAKE.

Interrogatory 1: State your name, residence, and what official position you hold in Barbour county.

Answer: My name is Reuben Lake; I reside at Lake City, Barbour county, Kansas; I am Sheriff of Barbour county.

Int. 2: State if you have heard the above statement of D. E. Sheldon read; and if so, state if it is in your opinion a correct statement of the facts connected with the Indian troubles as therein set forth.

Ans.: I have heard it read, and from what I know of all the circumstances connected with the Indian troubles in 1874, I believe it to be correct, and I indorse it as correct.

                    REUBEN LAKE.

STATE OF KANSAS, BARBOUR COUNTY, ss.

Reuben Lake, being duly sworn, says the foregoing statement, by him made, is correct and true, as he verily believes.

                    REUBEN LAKE.

Subscribed and sworn to before me, this 17th day of August, A. D. 1875.   D. VAN SLYKE,

[SEAL.]   *County Clerk, Barbour County, Kansas.*

STATEMENT OF JESSE MELTON AND C. M. BOUGHTON.

STATE OF KANSAS, BARBOUR COUNTY, ss.

Jesse Melton and Chas. M. Boughton, Deputy Clerk District Court, Barbour county, Kansas, being duly sworn, say that they have heard the foregoing statement of D. E. Sheldon read, and from their knowledge of the facts, said statement is true, as they verily believe.

JESSE MELTON.
C. M. BOUGHTON.

Subscribed and sworn to before me, this 18th day of August, A. D. 1875.

D. VAN SLYKE,

[SEAL.]   *County Clerk, Barbour County, Kansas.*

TESTIMONY OF WM. M. FRIEDLEY.

Interrogatory 1: State your name, residence, and what official position you hold in Barbour county, Kansas.

Answer: My name is Wm. M. Friedley; I reside in Barbour county, Kansas, in the town of Medicine Lodge; I am Probate Judge and Register of Deeds of Barbour county.

Int. 2: State if you have heard the statement of D. E. Sheldon read, setting forth the Indian troubles in 1874; and if so, state whether said statement contains a true account of said troubles, and if the facts therein set forth are reliable.

Ans.: I have heard said statement read. Many of the facts therein set forth I know to be true, and the whole statement is concise and entirely reliable, and I indorse it as correct. I heard S. J. Shepler say that the only reason he thought he was not scalped on the 6th of August, was because he had oxen, not horses or mules.

WM. M. FRIEDLEY.

STATE OF KANSAS, RENO COUNTY, ss.

Wm. M. Friedley, being duly sworn, says the above statement, by him made, is true and correct, as he verily believes.

WM. M. FRIEDLEY.

Subscribed and sworn to before me, this 20th day of August, A. D. 1875.

LEWIS HANBACK,

United States Commissioner, District of Kansas.

4

TESTIMONY OF E. W. ILIFF.

Interrogatory 1: State your name, place of residence, and occupation.

Answer: My name is Ezra W. Iliff; residence, Medicine Lodge, Barbour county, Kansas; occupation, herding. Have resided in Barbour county something over two years last past.

Int. 2: Were you a resident of Barbour county during the spring and summer of 1874? and if so, state what you know of the origin of the Indian troubles; and in this connection, state the condition of the settlers relative to their being in a continued state of alarm during that time.

Ans.: I was a resident of Barbour county during that time. All I know about the origin of the Indian troubles of that year (1874), is that there seemed all at once to be a preconcerted movement on the part of the Cheyennes, Arapahoes, Osages and other tribes along the border, organized for the purpose of committing depredations on our border; but there was but little attention paid to the matter until the 17th day of June, 1874, when three of our citizens, living at different points in Barbour county, Kansas, were killed and scalped by Indians. The men's names were Keim, Martin and Kennedy; Keim and Martin were men of families. Immediately on the reception of the news of these murders being had at Medicine Lodge, the greatest excitement prevailed; the settlers came flocking into town with their families and whatever stock they had, until there were probably 300 souls inside of the stockade. Active preparations were made for defense, and petitions and letters forwarded to the Governor of Kansas for assistance in the shape of provisions, arms and ammunition. Authority was given C. M. Ricker to raise a company of militia, and hold it in readiness for active service; which he immediately proceeded to do, and a company of about 60 men was organized. During all the rest of the months of June and July a constant state of alarm continued all along our border. Reports came in frequently of outrages committed by Indians, and whether true or not, served to keep all settlers from returning to their claims. During these months, the militia company, although not mustered in, was kept in constant duty, making frequent scouts, and always holding itself in readiness for instant service. All the reports of Indian incursions and depredations committed by them, fixed them on the Cheyennes,

Arapahoes and Osages, there being a difference of opinion as to which tribe or tribes they should be attributed to. There was one thing certain, however: the citizens in Medicine Lodge, as a general rule, fully believed that the Osages were leading spirits in the outrages committed.

Int. 3: State if you was a member of that portion of the company which moved out of Medicine Lodge under command of Captain Ricker on the morning of the 7th of August; and if so, state as clearly as you can what took place on that day.

Ans.: I was a member of that party, and the facts, as near as I can state them, are as follows: On the evening of the 6th of August, 1874, about 9 or 10 o'clock, our camp was aroused by S. J. Shepler, who brought in news that a body of Indians were in camp about 15 miles northeast from Medicine Lodge. Orders were given for 25 men, including officers, to prepare rations and be in readiness to march at daylight next day. On the morning of the next day, August 7th, the command marched in the direction indicated by Shepler. About 1 o'clock P. M., indications of Indians were discovered. The command halted, and Captain Ricker advanced to reconnoiter. We saw him returning, waving his hat, and we advanced towards him very fast. We saw two or three Indians coming towards us. That was the first we discovered them, and continued to advance upon the main party, who had then made their appearance, and were formed in something like a battle-line. Altogether we captured six prisoners. The main line still remained where it had originally been formed. Capt. Ricker and his men motioned for them to come up, which they refused to do. Whereupon Lieut. Moseley (who speaks and understands the Osage language), told one of the Indians to call to the Indians in the main line to come and give themselves up. The Indian, who represented himself as chief of the party, gave a call, and the Lieutenant sprang at him and told him if he (the Indian) told them to shoot at us again he (Moseley) would strike him with his gun. Immediately after this the Indians we had commenced trying to escape, and we were trying to prevent them; there was considerable commotion for a moment. As soon as it was evident that the Osages we had would escape, firing commenced, and the result was four Indians killed. A part of our command followed the main body for some distance, but without effect. In attempting to restrain one of the prisoners from escaping, I was struck with a club by him and knocked to my knees. The Indians were extremely insolent, refusing to give up their arms until compelled to do so, and absolutely refusing to dismount. One of the Indians, as he came up to our party, had his bow and arrow drawn. I had no doubt at that time that those Indians were there for hostile purposes, and not for collecting meat; that, I believe, was only a pretext. Their camp was concealed from view, except from one direction; their horses, etc., were in the brush, on the bank of the creek, and so concealed from view that we did not know they were there until we returned from the chase. From the best of my knowledge, there were twenty-seven warriors in the party. I am certain of this, having counted those who were in line. I am satisfied that there was but one woman in the party; there were no children. We found war paint on the persons of the Indians killed. The Indians that we saw were all painted; their hair and faces were painted, and so were some of their horses painted in large red stripes.

Int. 4: State if any demonstrations of violence were made by your party until after the chief told the Indians to fire, and the prisoners commenced trying to escape.

Ans.: No, sir; there was not—nothing more than would be given any prisoners captured in war. We treated them as prisoners, holding them under guard, and refusing to shake hands with them. The engagement was brought on by the acts of the Indians themselves.   E. W. ILIFF.

STATE OF KANSAS, BARBOUR COUNTY, ss.

E. W. Iliff, being duly sworn, says that he made the foregoing statement; that it has been read to him; that the facts therein set forth are true in substance and in fact, as he verily believes.

E. W. ILIFF.

Subscribed and sworn to before me, this 14th day of August, A. D. 1875.   D. VAN SLYKE,

[SEAL.]   *County Clerk, Barbour County, Kansas.*

TESTIMONY OF LEVI DAVIS.

Interrogatory 1: State your name, residence and occupation.

Answer: My name is Levi Davis; I reside at Kiowa, Barbour county, Kansas; my occupation is a farmer; I have lived in this county for about three years.

Int. 2: State what you know and have heard from reliable sources of any depredations being committed by Osage Indians.

Ans.: About the 3d of August, 1874, a band of Osages numbering from thirty-three to thirty-eight, came to Kiowa. I was at their camp, counted them as near as I could, and also counted and examined the animals, as I was looking for three horses which had strayed from me into the Osage nation some time before. I think I saw three women with them; no children. The Indians acted friendly to me. They said they were after buffalo. None of the horses I saw were painted. I saw but one young brave painted. Among these was one Indian with only one eye, who could talk English. The Indians remained there for a short time and then left, and I did not see them any more after they left. Prior to this time, say about three weeks, this same band, or a part of it, in the southern part of the county, captured four animals, two horses and two mules, from two citizens of Sumner county, and ran them off. The Indian with one eye was with this party. After taking the animals the band moved off in a westerly direction, crossing the Medicine Lodge about six miles below the town of Medicine Lodge, and kept on to the Salt Fork. The Indian with the one eye was killed by Capt. Ricker's command on the 7th of August, 1874. On the 16th of June, 1874, a party of Indians, I think Cheyennes, attacked Kiowa, and after firing into the town a large number of shots, left, taking with them four or five horses. During the latter part of June, July and August, the country known as Barbour county was in a constant state of alarm. It was apprehended that a general Indian war might ensue. All Indians were looked upon with suspicion, and every precaution was taken to prevent a surprise. By day and night the course of traveling bands of Indians was indicated by burning prairies. I do not believe there were more than from three to five squaws with the band at Kiowa.   **LEVI DAVIS.**

STATE OF KANSAS, BARBOUR COUNTY, ss.

Levi Davis, being duly sworn, says that the statement above set forth is true in substance and in fact, as he verily believes.

LEVI DAVIS.

Subscribed and sworn to before me, this 14th day of August, A. D. 1875.

[SEAL.]   D. VAN SLYKE,
                          County Clerk, Barbour County, Kansas.

TESTIMONY OF W. M. LAMPTON.

Interrogatory 1: State your name, residence and occupation.

Answer: My name is W. M. Lampton; I reside in Barbour county, Kansas; occupation, a farmer.

Int. 2: State if you was a member of Capt. C. M. Ricker's company of militia in August, 1874; and if so, state if you was present at a fight with the Osages in Barbour county, Kansas, on the 7th day of August, 1874; and in this connection give a full statement of all that occurred in that engagement.

Ans.: I was a member of that company at that time, and was present at the fight. The facts as they came under my notice are these: On the evening of August 6, 1874, Mr. S. J. Shepler came into our camp at Medicine Lodge, and brought information of a party of Indians being in camp about fifteen miles northeast from us. He was laboring under great excitement, and his news created an uproar and excitement in camp and through the town. Orders were immediately given for rations to be prepared for twenty-five men, and early next day we moved, under command of Capt. Ricker and Lieut. Moseley, in search of the Indians. Shortly after noon, Ricker's and Moseley's attention was called by me to what I took to be a camp; they doubted it was a camp, and started in advance of the command, taking different directions, for the purpose of reconnoitering. In a few moments we saw Ricker coming at a full run, waving his hat for us to come on, which we did, and when we met him we went on with him towards the camp, and pretty soon we met an Indian coming towards us; the first we saw he was close on to us. Ricker told him to dismount, and he took his bow away from him and told him to remount, which he did, and went on with us. We went up on top of next ridge, and the Indians formed a line of battle some 300 yards in front of us. Other Indians front of the Indian line and near our line came up to us (Ricker having motioned to them to do so). They were mounted and armed, and came up to us, all of them, with their bows strung and their arrows in their hands. They were disarmed as they came up. They were all insolent; their whole conduct indicated they were on the war-path, as Indians never carry their bows and arrows as these did unless they mean fight. I make this statement advisedly, as I have been on the plains since 1865, and am thoroughly acquainted with the habits of all the Indian tribes (the Osages included) which range along the Kansas frontier. In the meantime, and as we came up on top of the hill, we formed a line facing the Indian line. Our line extended for some distance, and all the Indians we had captured were on the right flank of the line. Myself and five or six others were ordered to dismount and hold ourselves in readiness for further orders; the rest of the line remained mounted, and was in plain view of the Indian line of battle. None of the Indians captured were in front of the mounted line. This state of affairs remained but a few moments, when Ricker and Moseley ordered the Indian who seemed to be chief to tell the Indians in line to come up. He hallooed to the Indians in line, speaking in Osage; when immediately Lieut. Moseley sprang towards him and said, "If you tell them to fire upon us again I will shoot hell out of you." As soon as Moseley said this the captured Indians commenced attempting to escape; one of them ran over Monroe Van Slyke, and one of them knocked E. W. Iliff down. We all thought that the fight had commenced, and that the Indians would fire upon us, so the firing commenced on our side, both at the Indians escaping from us and those in line. We followed them two or three miles, but did not fire any shots at them, as they were too far off. We returned, took the ponies, etc., left by the Indians, and returned to camp at Medicine Lodge, where we were received with demonstrations of joy. At no time before, during, or after, the fight, did we think we were murdering anybody. We treated the Indians as a war party, fully believing them to be hostile. Two horses and two of the Indians that I saw had the war paint on, and I am satisfied, and always have been, that this band was bent on mischief. There was only one woman in the band, that I saw; no children. If there had been any more I should have seen them. My judgment is that there were between thirty and forty Indians in the band. An Indian with one eye, who seemed to be a chief, was one of the slain. Lieut. Moseley, I am informed, talks and understands the Osage language. My impression, at the time of the fight, was that the Indians fired first; it was all excitement on both sides, and the affair was over in a few moments.   WM. M. LAMPTON.

STATE OF KANSAS, BARBOUR COUNTY, ss.

Wm. M. Lampton, being duly sworn, says the foregoing statement, by him made, is true in substance and in fact, as he verily believes.   WM. M. LAMPTON.

Subscribed and sworn to before me, this 16th day of August, 1875.   D. VAN SLYKE,

[SEAL.]   *County Clerk, Barbour County, Kansas.*

TESTIMONY OF CHARLES C. BOND.

Interrogatory 1: State your name, residence and occupation.

Answer: My name is Charles C. Bond; residence, Barbour county, Kansas; occupation, a physician.

Int. 2: State if you ever had any encounter with any Indians. If so, state when as near as you can, with what tribe, and state in this connection all the circumstances that transpired at that time.

Ans.: I have. Early on one morning in the fore part of the month of July, 1874. I was going from my house to the town of Sun City, in Barbour county. Just before daylight, and while still at my house, I was aroused by the barking of my dog. Got up, supposing some persons were in my watermelon patch. I took my gun, listened a while, fired it off, and I listened a moment and heard the cracking of the brush as some parties ran away. I afterwards examined the ground and found moccasin tracks, showing that Indians had been there, undoubtedly after my two horses, which were tied one at each corner of the house. After I started and had gone about two miles, I heard dogs at

Mr. Carl's house barking; could not imagine what was the matter. I kept on my way, when suddenly I saw to my left hand (*i. e.*, south of me) some horsemen. At first I supposed they were some of our militia stationed at Lake City, but on second look I made up my mind that they were Indians. They were coming in single file and on the run, and almost immediately after I saw they were Indians, the one in advance fired upon me. My horse as I got off from him sheered a little to my left. I drew my revolver (a Remington) and fired at the last one of them (there being four in the party). He fired at the same time at me. We both missed. This was the second shot. Immediately after I got the third shot. I then started to run for the brush close by; had gone a short distance when I got the fourth shot. As I got to the edge of the brush I got the fifth shot; and so on until seven shots were fired at me. I proceeded rapidly and soon came across some of our men stationed at Lake City, near by, who hearing the shots had started on foot to see what the matter was. I told them to go back and get their horses, which they did, and we all went back to where the melee had taken place. The Indians were gone. Myself and another man went up to Carl's house, and found the family had left. The Indians retreated south and escaped, taking with them three horses belonging to Mr. Abraham Winnie and one from William Carl. I am certain that the party that attacked me were Indians. The one I fired at was within twenty-five feet of me. They were all in plain view of me and I of them. I am certain, from what I know myself and from information which I have received from persons who are acquainted with Indian signs and habits, and on whose judgment I rely, that they were Osage Indians. After the horses captured by Capt. Ricker in the fight with the Osages on the 7th day of August, 1874, were brought into Medicine Lodge, I saw one of the horses, and I am certain that it was the same animal that the Indian who shot at me first rode. I believe so because of the very peculiar make of the animal, so much so as would attract the attention and fix the memory of any person looking at it. A portion of the militia at Sun City followed the trail of the retreating Indians, but failed to come up with them; and one Robert Espy, who resides in Lake City township and was engaged in the pursuit, found on the trail a woman's scalp, covered with long hair, which had undoubtedly been lost by this party. The scalp is now in the possession of parties in Barbour county.   DR. C. C. BOND.

STATE OF KANSAS, BARBOUR COUNTY, ss.

Charles C. Bond, being duly sworn, says that the foregoing statement by him made is true in substance and in fact, as he verily believes.   DR. C. C. BOND.

Subscribed and sworn to before me, this 16th day of August, A. D. 1875.

    [SEAL.]   D. VAN SLYKE,
           County Clerk, Barbour County, Kansas.

STATEMENT OF DR. T. W. DAVIS.

Interrogatory 1: State your name, residence, and what official position you hold.

Answer: My name is T. W. Davis; I reside at Medicine Lodge, Barbour county, Kansas; I am a physician, and am also Justice of the Peace of Medicine Lodge township.

Int. 2: State if you was at Kiowa, in this county, in the early part of August, 1874, at the time a party of Osages were there; and if so, state what you know of the circumstances connected with their visit.

Ans.: I was there on the 5th day of August to see a patient; I arrived there a few moments after a company of the Sixth Cavalry, United States Army, had returned from chasing what they said was a party of Osages. I talked with a Government scout in the employ of the Government troops; he said that they had been following them for a number of miles, and that they were ordered to drive them, and all other Indians, out of the State, who were in the State without authority. He said that they had come in sight of a band of Osages that day, and had chased them, and had followed them, I believe, three or four miles east of the Medicine; and that they were pressing them pretty hard, and they separated and scattered in every direction, and they (the troops) had given up the chase; and the commander of the company said they were going back to Dodge after supplies. At the same day and place, Mr. Sparks, one of the citizens of Kiowa, came in from the east off a buffalo hunt, and came through, or by, those Osage Indians, twelve or fifteen miles east of Kiowa; and he said the Indians acted insolent and unfriendly. He stated they were Osages. Davis, and others at Kiowa, said that three of them came up to the house, or near it, and talked a little; but they acted sullen and insolent. I came home the next day, and reported what I had heard to Captain Ricker and others. The same evening Shepler came in with his report, and the next morning the militia went out and had the fight. Previous to this time, I. T. Gibson, Agent of the Osages, was here. He said he was on the hunt of Osages; he said there was then one band (I believe it was Black Dog's band) that was out, and that they had left the reservation contrary to his advice or consent; and that he believed them to be west of this, and that he was afraid that if they came across the Cheyennes or Kiowas that they would join their war parties; that he believed if he could see them that he could induce them to go back to the reservation. He tried here to get conveyance and an escort to go to their camp, or to hunt them wherever they were; and he was not able to obtain either conveyance or escort, and he left, saying he was going to Wichita. He manifested a good deal of uneasiness for fear they would join the Cheyennes or Kiowas. I was fully acquainted with the condition of affairs relative to the Indian difficulties during that time; there was a general feeling of fear prevalent throughout the whole county. The country was given up; nearly everybody was in the towns inside the stockades. A state of war actually existed, and when the command under Captain Ricker marched out from Medicine Lodge, we that remained behind believed they were going for our protection, to meet hostile, not peaceable, Indians, and we hoped they would drive them beyond the limits of the State. When Shepler came in that day, August 6th, he was very much excited; he represented that he was afraid of the Indians, and that he did not go to them, or talk to them. My recollection of Frank Shepler's (S. J. Shepler's son, who was with him) account of seeing the Indians is this: He said him and his father saw the Indians on the side of a hill, or one side of the road, and they (Shepler and son) sheered off on one side, kept right on and did not allow the Indians to come near them. I don't know whether he stated that the Indians attempted to come near them or not. T. W. DAVIS.

TESTIMONY OF ELI SMITH.

Interrogatory 1: What is your name, residence and occupation?

Answer: Eli Smith; residence, Kiowa, Barbour county, Kansay; occupation, a farmer.

Int. 2: State what you know about the town of Kiowa being attacked by Indians on the 16th of June, 1874, or about that time.

Ans: On the 16th of June, 1874, the town of Kiowa was attacked by Indians. None of the citizens were killed, but there were some narrow escapes. A large number of shots were fired into the town, and after a time the Indians retreated, taking with them some three or four horses. They left about 5 o'clock P. M., and camped on Mule creek. From all I can learn I am confident this is the same party which surprised and murdered Martin, Kennedy and Keim, on the 17th. The whole country was immediately thrown into a great state of alarm; people left their claims and flocked into the towns; all business was suspended, at least to a great extent, and as a matter of fact a complete state of war existed. It was considered unsafe for a white man to travel the country unprotected, and it was equally unsafe for an Indian of any tribe to be found within the borders of the State. This state of affairs continued for several months. Immediately after the 16th and 17th of June, the citizens commenced arming and organizing for defense. A militia company was formed. I was Lieutenant in command of the detachment stationed at Kiowa. The rest of the company was stationed at Medicine Lodge. The whole company was composed of honest, intelligent and peaceable citizens. A great many of the members of the company were heads of families. On the 2d or 3d of August, 1874, a band of Osages numbering over thirty men, one or two squaws at most, and two boys about thirteen years old, camped near the town of Kiowa. I went down into their camp and examined it. I found rifles and pistols (revolvers), the latter mostly packed; but few arms were shown me; the bows and arrows were mostly packed. I tried to talk to the Indians in English, but with little effect. I told them in words and by signs which they understood (as some of them could talk English), to go back, in fact ordered them to go back — we did not want them in the country — but they would only say, "Heap buffalo coming," and pointed southeast, and they wanted to go northeast from Kiowa so as to catch them. I am positive there were not more than two squaws along with the party.   There were many things which made me suspicious of the band.   One was, they kept as nearly as possible their arms concealed; another was, they would not talk English; another was, one of the braves was painted, his horse was painted, he (the Indian) was armed with a shield, and he was in every respect gotten up in war style; besides, he was insolent in his manner and bearing.   I do not think that this band of Osages was an actual war party; that is, actually organized for war, but I am confident that they meant trouble, and were in the country not for buffalo but for scalps and robbery.   In fact, Mahlon Stubbs, agent of the Kaw Indians, stated to me in Medicine Lodge, Kansas, in presence of John Moseley, in front of Judge Updegraff's house, that this band was a mourning party, and I have no doubt they were on a mission of blood, not peace.   Among these Indians was a one-eyed Indian who could talk English.   I tried to talk with him, but he paid no attention to me, pretending he could not understand, as I took it.   We left him and the party, and the next day I came over to Medicine Lodge to make my report to Capt. Ricker.

ELI SMITH.

STATE OF KANSAS, BARBOUR COUNTY, ss.

Eli Smith, being duly sworn, says the statements contained in the foregoing are true in substance and in fact, as he verily believes.   ELI SMITH.

Subscribed and sworn to before me, this 16th day of August, A. D. 1875.

[SEAL.]

D. VAN SLYKE,
County Clerk, Barbour County, Kansas.

TESTIMONY OF DARIUS VAN SLYKE.

Interrogatory 1: State your name, residence, and what official position you now hold.

Answer: My name is Darius Van Slyke; residence, Medicine Lodge, Barbour county, Kansas; I am Postmaster of Medicine Lodge, and County Clerk of Barbour county.

Int. 2: State if you was a member of Captain C. M. Ricker's company, of Barbour county, and if you was present at a fight

with the Osages on the 7th day of August, 1874; and if so, state
all that occurred under your observation.

Ans.: I was a member of that company; I was present at the
fight of August 7, 1874, with the Osages.   The facts of the fight
are substantially as follows: On the night of the 6th, I understood that Shepler had come in with information that he had
seen Indians northeast of this place, about fifteen or sixteen
miles.   My understanding was that Shepler and his son (who
was with him) were frightened when they came in.   Twenty-five
of us were ordered to prepare to go out on the 7th, to see what
the Indians were there for.   And on the next morning we went
out; traveled in a northeast direction about twelve miles, and
we camped and ate dinner.   We then went on, and about three
miles we discovered what some of us supposed was the Indian
camp; I believe Captain Ricker thought it was dead cottonwood
logs, and he and Lieut. Moseley went out to reconnoiter, Ricker
going one way and Moseley another.   After Ricker had been
absent a short time, we saw him coming towards us on the run,
swinging his hat.   We started on and met him, and advanced towards the camp, when we saw one Indian coming towards us.
When we met him Ricker ordered him to dismount, and took his
bow and arrow from him.   About this time another Indian
came over the hill and was disarmed, and from that more came
stringing in, until there were six, who were disarmed; two of
them had guns and one a revolver, the rest had bows and arrows.   They were backward about giving up their arms, and
one or two refused to until Ricker spoke cross to them, and told
them to give them up.   By this time about twenty Indians
(mounted) came on the hill, and formed a line about three hundred yards from us.   We formed a line and advanced a short
distance towards them, they still maintaining their line.   We
halted, and Ricker told one of the Indians, who was a sort of a
chief, to call to the Indians in line to come up.   The chief hallooed back at the other Indians in the Osage language, when
immediately Lieut. Moseley, who speaks and understands the
Osage language, jumped towards him and told him "if he told
the Indians to fire on us again he would mash or knock his
brains out," or words to that effect.   Whereupon the captured
Indians, who were mounted, immediately tried to escape.   E. W.
Iliff had hold of one of the ponies, when the Indian on the pony
commenced beating him over the head with a heavy club, some-

thing like a "quirtz," used by the Indians. There was great excitement in ours and the Indian lines; we saw rapid movements on their part, for what purpose we did not know. So far as I was concerned, and those around me, we supposed a battle had commenced and we commenced firing. I was on the east part of the line; the Indians captured were on the west end of the line. They made a desperate effort to escape, and in the attempt four, as we afterwards ascertained, were killed. It was my impression at the time that the Indians in line fired at us; some of the men claimed that they heard balls whistle close to them. The whole fight or melee was over inside of two minutes. The Indians retreated as fast as they could; a part of our command gave chase; I was with the chase. No shots were fired by us after we started, as the Indians were too far in advance. We followed two or three miles, and gave up the chase and returned to the Indian camp. Up to this time the main portion of our command had no knowledge of any horses, mules or ponies being secreted by the Indians in the brush, but when we returned we were informed by some of our men who had remained behind, that there were some fifty and over horses, mules and ponies found. We took possession of them, and brought them with us to Medicine Lodge, where an inventory was made of them, and a report forwarded to the Adjutant General of Kansas, at Topeka. So far as I was concerned, I believed at the time that this was a war party of Osages, and I believe so now. I think their hunting meat was only a pretext. The Indians that came to us were painted, and one of the horses was painted in stripes. I know John Moseley well; he is a man of good standing here; is a man of truth. Understanding, as he does, the Osage language, I believe he interpreted it truthfully when he ordered the chief not to tell the line again to fire on us. I believe now, and did then, that the Indian did tell his party to fire on us, probably for the purpose of aiding them in making their escape. The Indians could fire upon a greater part of our line without injuring the captured Indians, and it is my impression they did fire on our part of the line. I have heard read a copy of Mahlon Stubbs's report to the President's Peace Commission, who was a member of a commission who came here in August, 1874, to investigate the affair of August 7th. It is in the main ungenerous and untrue. The Commission was treated in the best way possible; there was no insult or indignity offered them. We tried to make it pleasant for them; but when they told us if we did not give up the ponies they were afraid the Indians would come up and clean us out, we told them to send them on. The report by said Stubbs, in my judgment, emanates from an improper purpose; a purpose to create a prejudice and false impression in the minds of the Indian authorities against the citizens of Barbour county. In fact, there has been a continued effort on the part of Agent Gibson, Superintendent Hoag, and others connected with the Indian affairs on the border, to get at a state of facts as favorable to the Indians and as unfavorable and prejudicial to the whites, as possibly could be done. I know a Mr. Rankin, who was here to obtain testimony in January last. He came here; remained several days; did not make known his business any more than he could help; did not consult the citizens generally, so as to arrive at the truth of the affair; but took affidavits of several who were not in the fight, among whom was Shepler, who first gave the alarm, and those whose affidavits were taken who were in the fight (had with the Osages) were mostly enemies of Ricker: Henry Moore, the Sheplers, Tip McClure, were dropped from the roll of the company for various reasons. Rankin seemed to seek for those citizens who were disaffected with the turn of affairs in this county. Added to all this, there were internal dissensions in the county, out of which have grown two parties. Now, however, such a state of affairs does not exist. In conclusion, I say emphatically that the militia company at this place was organized out of the citizens of this town and the surrounding country, solely for the purpose of defending their homes and property. Murder and plunder were not its prime or remote objects. It was considered that a state of war existed; all Indians found in our county were looked upon as hostile; there was no middle ground in the matter when men—good citizens and neighbors, following the peaceful avocations of life—were murdered and scalped almost within sight of our town. When we marched on the 7th of August, we believed we were after hostile Indians, and I believe so now.　　　　　D. VAN SLYKE.

UNITED STATES OF AMERICA, DISTRICT OF KANSAS, ss.

Darius Van Slyke, being duly sworn, says the foregoing state-

www.ingramcontent.com/pod-product-compliance
Lightning Source LLC
Chambersburg PA
CBHW021536270326
41930CB00008B/1282